The Tragic Daughters of Charles I

The Tragic Daughters of Charles I

Sarah-Beth Watkins

Winchester, UK
Washington, USA

First published by Chronos Books, 2019
Chronos Books is an imprint of John Hunt Publishing Ltd., No. 3 East St., Alresford,
Hampshire SO24 9EE, UK
office1@jhpbooks.net
www.johnhuntpublishing.com

For distributor details and how to order please visit the 'Ordering' section on our website.

ISBN: 978 1 78904 113 2
978 1 78904 114 9 (ebook)
Library of Congress Control Number: 2018942987

A CIP catalogue record for this book is available from the British Library.

Design: Stuart Davies

Printed and bound by CPI Group (UK) Ltd, Croydon, CR0 4YY, UK

We operate a distinctive and ethical publishing philosophy in
all areas of our business, from our global network of authors to
production and worldwide distribution.

Contents

Prologue

On a cold winter's morning King Charles I was led from St James Palace to Whitehall by the New Model Army, their drums beating along the route. It was so cold the Thames had frozen over and Charles wore two shirts to keep out the chill. At Whitehall the king prayed and took a drink of claret. Quietly composed, he awaited his fate.

Huge crowds had gathered but were kept back from the scaffold that had been prepared for the execution of a king. He had prepared a speech but was worried that no one would hear him so he directed his words to those that were witnesses at the scaffold:

> I have forgiven all the world, and even those in particular that have been the chief causes of my death. Who they are, God knows, I do not desire to know, God forgive them. But this is not all, my charity must go further. I wish that they may repent, for indeed they have committed a great sin in that particular. I pray God, with St. Stephen, that this be not laid to their charge. Nay, not only so, but that they may take the right way to the peace of the kingdom, for my charity commands me not only to forgive particular men, but my charity commands me to endeavour to the last gasp the Peace of the Kingdom. So, Sirs, I do wish with all my soul, and I do hope there is some here (turning to some gentlemen that wrote) that will carry it further, that they may endeavour the peace of the Kingdom.[1]

A soldier interrupted his speech when he stumbled against the axe and Charles told him 'Hurt not the axe that may hurt me' fearing it may become blunt. He continued addressing the witnesses until another man did the same and he said 'Take heed of the axe, pray, take heed of the axe'.[2]

When he was ready the king turned to the executioner said,

'I shall say but very short prayers, and when I thrust out my hands...' He was passed his nightcap and had help to tuck in his mass of dark curls away from his neck. He told the gathered men 'I go from a corruptible, to an incorruptible Crown; where no disturbance can be, no disturbance in the World'.[3]

Taking off his cloak, he checked with the executioner that his hair was out of the way and removed his doublet and waistcoat before replacing his cloak. He asked the executioner whether the block could be higher but it could not. The king placed his head on the block and asked the executioner to wait for the sign. When he stretched forward his hands, the axe fell and Charles I lost his head in one stroke. It was held aloft with the words 'behold the head of a traitor'.[4]

He left behind him his queen Henrietta Maria, his sons, Charles, James and Henry and his daughters Mary, Elizabeth, Anne and Henrietta Anne. The king's daughters, these Stuart princesses, would lead short, troubled lives. This is their story.

Chapter One

The Stuart Family

1631–1642

The married life of King Charles I of England and Henrietta Maria of France was destined to be tumultuous. Their relationship would be set against years of civil war, political upheaval and bloodshed. As a family they would be driven apart and their children would be forced to face their own destinies. The couple would have four sons and five daughters yet two of their children would be stillborn. Of the four surviving daughters, Mary, Elizabeth, Anne and Henrietta Anne, only three lived into their teenage years and not one of them would reach their thirties.

This ill-fated royal couple married by proxy in May 1625 in a Catholic ceremony in front of the Notre Dame in Paris with the Duke of Chevreuse standing in as bridegroom. The notorious George Villiers, the Duke of Buckingham, was supposed to fill in for Charles but due to the death of King James, his journey was delayed. Buckingham had been the king's favourite since Charles was fourteen. They had hated each other at first but now he was the new king's right-hand man and as such would have a huge influence on his marriage.

Henrietta Maria would rue the day she met him even though he had 'so much charm and magnificence that he won the admiration of all the people. The ladies of the court were filled with joy (and something more than joy); the court gallants were openly envious; and all the husbands at court were consumed with jealousy'.[1] But already they had argued over her greeting the papal legate.

Henrietta Maria, daughter of Henry IV and Marie de Medici, had been brought up as a Catholic and she would never sway

3

in her beliefs. Her marriage treaty had included secret promises that Charles would end the persecution of Catholics in England and she had sworn to her mother and the Pope to help put a stop to their suffering. The least she could do was greet the papal representative in Paris but Buckingham could see trouble brewing.

In June the fifteen-year-old Henrietta sailed across the Channel with her huge entourage including twenty-eight Catholic priests and began her married life in her new country. Charles I met her at Dover and they travelled on to Canterbury for another wedding ceremony. She was described as being 'of a more lovely and lasting complexion, a dark brown; she hath eyes that sparkle like stars, and for her physiognomy she may be said to be a mirror of perfection'.[2] But she also had a fierce temper and would soon show she was unhappy with Charles and his favourite.

Her religion immediately caused problems as Buckingham had foreseen. Where was the chapel Charles had promised to have built for her? Her priests complained to the king and were told they could say Mass in the Great Chamber 'and if the Great Chamber were not wide enough, they might use the garden; and if the garden would not serve their turn, then was the park the fittest place'.[3] He angered Charles further by refusing to attend the ceremonies of the Order of the Garter – a Protestant ceremony and now there was the problem of their coronation.

Charles and Henrietta Maria's coronation ceremony was to take place in Westminster Abbey, an Anglican church, which posed a dilemma to Henrietta and her Catholic French advisers. It was suggested perhaps that the ceremony could take place outside the building with a Catholic priest officiating but any change to the coronation ceremony was unheard of. Charles had no intention of breaking with tradition and continued with his plans regardless of his new wife's wishes. In the end Henrietta didn't even attend the ceremony but watched the procession from a nearby house. She was never crowned which would lead to many believing she was not a true queen of England and would pose her problems in the future.

As a sign of the troubles to come in their relationship and across the country they would reign, Lucy Hutchinson wrote 'he (Charles I) married a Papist, a French lady of a haughty spirit and great wit and beauty, to whom he became a most uxorious husband. By this means the court was replenished with Papists, and many who hoped to advance themselves by the change turned to that religion'.[4]

It was an uneasy start to their marriage that was peppered by many quarrels, not helped by Buckingham always taking the king's side. Charles grew tired of Henrietta's prayers, piety and abstinence which threatened the succession. He felt she was being governed by her ill advisors and was determined to send them all back to France. Arriving at her chamber in Whitehall, he ordered they remove to Somerset House from where arrangements would be made for their return to their homeland. The Comtesse de Tillières, the queen's companion, reported that Henrietta 'almost died, crying out, despairing, demanding us back with such prayers and tears that if it had been another [man than Charles] assuredly we would have been called back'.[5] But Charles would not back down and Henrietta threw herself against the window, banging her fists against the glass as the servants left the building, blood running down her little hands whilst her women 'howled and lamented, as if they were going to execution'.[6]

Henrietta Maria was in a world of misery and finally Charles allowed just twenty of her people to stay but their relationship was fraught. During the months that would pass it would have its ups and downs until a tragedy brought them together. The Duke of Buckingham had been overseeing the relief of Huguenots in La Rochelle and the unsuccessful capture of the Île de Ré fortified by French troops. While he organised another campaign from Portsmouth he was stabbed by a disgruntled army officer, John Felton, and died crying out 'Villain' It was a tragedy for his family and Charles who so depended on him but it would bring the king and Henrietta Maria closer together as she helped him mourn his loss. Finally after all these years, they grew to love one another and Henrietta Maria would be fiercely devoted to her husband and committed to his cause as their fortunes changed over the coming years.

And their renewed relationship meant Henrietta soon became pregnant. Her first child was born prematurely after a problematic breech labour when the king was asked whether to save the mother or the child and said 'he could have other children, please God'.[7] Their next son, Charles, heir to the throne, would arrive without difficulty in 1630.

Mary was their first daughter born 4 November 1631 at a time of peace at St James' Palace, a stunning red brick mansion built in the reign of Henry VIII. Henrietta Maria worried whether this baby would survive and she was baptised immediately although some said the ceremony had been kept low key to save money. Either way, under the administrations of Dr Mayerne, this first daughter and Princess Royal rallied and was cared for by her nurses Mrs Bennett and Mrs Griffin under Countess Roxburgh's supervision in the nursery at St James' Palace. Here, with her older brother, they were supported by a household of servants from pages to dressmakers and in time Monsieur d'Aranjon, their French and writing master. A brother James joined them in 1633 and then a second daughter Elizabeth in 1635 named after her godmother, the Queen of Bohemia. Unlike her dark-haired sister Mary, she was more fair-haired like her mother. Elizabeth was born in the midst of a snow laden winter earning her the name 'the winter princess'. At her baptism officiated by Archbishop Laud, the Prince Palatine stood as her godfather.

Plague broke out in the city the following year and the Stuart children were all moved to Richmond, the beautiful palace and gardens by the Thames, where the air was cleaner. Their parents spent the summer with them before the court moved to Oxford in the autumn. Cold winter months saw the plague recede and the king and queen return to London. Countess Roxburgh took Mary and Elizabeth to court in the spring of 1637 and during their visit another daughter was born to add to the nursery. Anne was baptised with her brother Charles and sister Mary as godparents before the Countess took them back to the safety and tranquillity of Richmond. In August they attended the wedding of James Stuart, Duke of Richmond and Lennox to Mary Villiers at York House. All who saw the lovely girls were delighted by their impeccable manners and courteous behaviour. They were the model of a happy royal family.

But as with any family tensions lay under the surface. Religion would always be an issue between Charles and his wife although Henrietta Maria now had her own chapel. The children were baptised in the Anglican Church but the queen would rather they be brought up in the Catholic faith and over the years would press her children to convert. Taking Elizabeth to an evening service, the two-year-old became restless and was given a book of devotions to quiet her. Seeing a picture of Jesus being whipped, she kissed the picture crying 'Poor man! Poor man!' to her mother's delight.

In the winter of 1638 Henrietta Maria's mother, Marie de Medici arrived in England. Only her daughter was happy to see her. Her troubles with her son King Louis XIII at the French court were such that Charles I did not want to get involved with such a formidable woman. Others were wary of this expensive guest who cost the treasury £3000 a month in her suite of fifty rooms at St James' Palace. Louis was more than happy 'for the King of Great Britain to have the entire charge of this hospitality, although he did not invite his guest'.[8] Henrietta Maria greeted her mother with much emotion witnessed by her children who were taken to greet the grandmother they had never met. Before she sailed for England, Marie had been at The Hague where she discussed the marriage of her granddaughter Elizabeth to William, son of the Prince of Orange. Again Charles did not want to get involved. For now he felt that such a marriage would be beneath his daughter.

Henrietta gave birth to another daughter Catherine in January 1639 but after a long and hard labour, the baby did not survive. The queen's mother at least was there to comfort her but the times were changing. Political unrest meant that whilst Charles I travelled to the North, Henrietta Maria, her mother and the children were all told to stay at Whitehall guarded by the city militia. The seeds of the English Civil War were beginning to grow around them. Still Henrietta Maria became pregnant again and in July 1640, her last son, Henry, Duke of Gloucester, was born. His brothers Charles and James stood as his godfathers and Mary made her first public appearance at eight years old to be his godmother. With the joy of his birth came a sadness just four months later when Anne their youngest daughter died in November at Richmond of tuberculosis.

Since coming to the throne in 1625, the king's reign had been one of change causing increasing instability and tension. Many of his policies were unpopular but Charles was strongly opinionated and confident in his choices feeling he was destined to hold supreme authority. The Bishops' Wars prompted by his introduction of a Book of Common Prayer in 1637 did nothing to improve his popularity and near bankrupted the crown. His comment 'I will rather die than yield to those impertinent and damnable demands; for it is all one as to yield to be no king in a very short time',[9] referring to the Covenanter's requests, would continue to be his attitude until the end.

The coming years would see his break with parliament plunge the country into civil war as the two sides, Royalist and Parliamentarian, made their stands. A contemporary would write 'we have insensibly slid into the beginning of a civil war by one unexpected accident after another, as waves of the sea which have brought us thus far and we scarce know how'.[10]

By now Charles I needed an alliance and he needed funds. In January 1641 he welcomed a delegation of Dutch ambassadors from The Hague to discuss the marriage of his daughter but instead of it being to Elizabeth as previously mooted, they requested Mary for their fifteen-year-old prince. Henrietta Maria was appalled. She had hopes that her eldest daughter would be married to a royal Roman Catholic prince – someone like Philip IV of Spain's son – but Charles could now see advantages in a marriage to Prince William. The Dutch promised him money, the possibility of military aid and even mediation with his disaffected parliament. And even Henrietta came round to the idea telling an ambassador that Prince Frederic Henry of Orange could provide them with 20,000 men. But others were not so happy with the match and wondered why the king would marry his daughter to a family without royal blood. Henrietta's family in France thought it disgraceful the Princess Royal should marry beneath herself.

Mary it was said was so 'fixed and grounded'[11] in the Protestant religion anyway she would only marry a Protestant prince but in reality she would do as her father bid her. At nine years old she would have no say in the matter. When asked if she agreed to the marriage she replied 'Yes, since the queen my mother desires it; and I wish the prince would come to England that we might meet'.[12]

Charles however did ensure that Mary was well looked after by the terms of her marriage treaty. Prince William had to travel to England for the wedding ceremony and she was to stay in England until she was twelve. She would be allowed twenty-six male and fourteen female servants picked by her father and in case of any vacancies arising, these would be filled by other English servants. Her dowry was £40,000 to be paid in four instalments and apart from her travel to The Hague, the Dutch were to cover all her costs plus pay her a yearly allowance of £1,500. She would also be allowed to worship as per Anglican Church rites and doctrines and not have to follow the tenets of the Dutch reformed church.

With those details agreed, Mary's marriage was planned for 2 May and the fifteen-year-old William arrived on 19 April 1641 at Gravesend, after a stormy journey in which the mast of ship was broken, with a train of fifty carriages. The next day as he passed by the Tower of London, he received a hundred-gun salute before reaching Whitehall. He was at first greeted by Charles and James who escorted him to the king and queen who he presented with gifts of jewels but it was not till the afternoon that he met his intended bride at Somerset House. He had not been permitted to kiss his bride-to-be and now was only allowed to kiss Mary's hand and not her face. Still he made a favourable impression. He was handsome, impeccably mannered, and wealthy. He was well-bred and well-educated, speaking five languages – English, Dutch, French, Spanish and Italian. He may not have royal blood but he was a catch.

And he was there to woo Mary. In the days leading up to their marriage he stayed in the house of the Earl of Arundel and visited her frequently at Somerset House with gifts of jewels using a key he was given to enter through the garden door.

Their wedding took place on 2 May 1641 with the Bishop of Ely officiating in the Chapel Royal. William wore 'rich crimson velvet, with a Vandyke collar of deep point lace'[13] and was accompanied by Count Brederode and other nobles from his entourage. Mary wore a robe of silver tissue adorned with a huge diamond brooch – a gift from William – with silver ribbons in her hair. Sixteen young ladies dressed in white satin carried her train as she approached the altar flanked by her brothers Charles and James where her father gave her away. Her mother Henrietta Maria, grandmother Marie de Medici and sister

Elizabeth watched from a private closet.

After the service, the newlyweds were escorted to the Queen's chamber for a royal blessing and later in the day they shared a family dinner followed by a walk in Hyde Park. Given Mary's age they were not to spend the night together but did take part in a bedding ceremony. The Princess Royal was undressed and donning a long nightgown lay on a bed draped with blue velvet curtains. William joined her in his dressing gown and was finally allowed to kiss her 'in the presence of all the great lords and ladies of England, the four ambassadors of the United [Dutch] States, and the distinguished personages who had attended him to London'.[14] Mary's nightgown was so long it hindered their touching of legs which would signify the consummation of their marriage. Henrietta's dwarf Geoffrey Hudson gleefully slit her gown with shears and pronounced the wedding ceremonies complete. William was then escorted to the king's bedchamber for the night.

But there was an unhappy guest at the wedding. Charles' nephew, Charles Louis, Prince Palatine, was telling anyone that would listen that Mary was promised to him although he had never been considered as a match. The Venetian ambassador reported 'The resentment of the Prince Palatine against the Prince of Orange over this marriage in no wise abates, and he does not trouble to hide his feelings. He has not called upon the bridegroom, and although invited he would not assist at the banquet with their Majesties and the wedded pair on the day of the marriage'.[15]

There were also no joyous celebrations in the city afterwards and for a royal wedding the whole affair had been muted coming at a time when the people were baying for the blood of Charles' advisor, the Earl of Strafford, who had been on trial for high treason. Ten thousand people had marched on Whitehall with a petition of 20,000 signatures calling for his death. Strafford was accused of being 'a main instrument to provoke the king to make a war between us and the Scots'[16] of raising troops in Ireland to quash Charles' enemies and making way for 'the papist party'. He had only ever been loyal to his king but Parliament wanted peace and they wanted his head. Whilst Mary was getting married, a plot to spring Strafford from the Tower was underway but with a lack of men and rumours spreading it was called off. Strafford was put on trial but even though the evidence proved inconclusive, a bill of attainder was put in front of Charles to sign condemning his advisor to death but the king could not bring himself to sign it. Strafford however could see how parliament was turning against their king. If Charles did not act with authority he would lose it and so the earl wrote to the king 'To set your Majesty's conscience at liberty, I do most humbly beseech your Majesty (for preventing evils which may happen by your refusal) to pass this bill'.[17]

Charles signed and his chief advisor was executed on Tower Hill on 12 May but the king would forever regret what he had done. The Venetian ambassador reported 'this minister lost his life whose admirable qualities certainly deserved a better age and a happier fate. The king, thus deprived of authority with the hatred of the people, which is even stronger against the queen... suffers the tortures of the deepest affliction'.[18] Despite Strafford's warning, the king's hold over his kingdom was waning.

Against this gloomy background William paid court to Mary. William was happy at least with his new bride when he wrote to his parents 'although we were at first very solemn towards each other, now we feel more at ease... I love her very much and I believe that she loves me too'.[19] Perhaps the prince could see the tide turning against the king of England or perhaps he just wanted to return to Holland with his new wife because William asked for permission for the Princess Royal to leave with him at the end of May. Charles refused. She was still too young and should remain in England for the next three years as per their marriage treaty. Only months later Charles would change his mind.

But for now the prince was leaving and he was presented with gifts to take home including a sword embellished with diamonds. Mary too gave him a jewelled brooch which he immediately pinned on his chest, and roses made from silver ribbon were presented to the Dutch ambassadors. She also wrote to her new father-in-law to tell him she was looking forward to meeting him. As William left the Tower by barge for Gravesend a gun salute sounded his departure. Mary wished to send him one last gift and tasked Sir Peter Killigrew with delivering an embroidered scarf to her husband at Deal in Kent from where he was to sail but by the time Killigrew arrived, the prince had already left. Unperturbed Killigrew took the next boat and Mary's gift soon found its recipient.

By July ill will towards the queen and her fellow Catholics made Charles worry for her safety. Henrietta Maria was blamed for trying to raise funds for the Bishops' War from fellow Catholics and members of Parliament were looking for a legal way to bring the queen to trial.

Perhaps she could take Mary to Holland after all and travel on to take the waters at Spa. This Charles put to Parliament who called in Dr Mayerne who pronounced Henrietta sick in mind and body and not likely to live long. The waters however had proved beneficial to her before and he recommended she take them again. Parliament were not convinced and saw behind it an excuse for Henrietta to travel abroad troublemaking, as they saw it, and rallying support for the king. Mary too was not allowed to leave. But someone they would see pleased to go, Marie de Medici, was making plans for her voyage back to France.

Charles left his family in safety at Oatlands in Surrey whilst he travelled to Scotland to smooth over recent events and win support. The queen was severely depressed and wrote to her sister 'I swear to you that I am driven almost mad by the sudden change in my fortunes. From the highest point of happiness I have fallen into despair… Imagine what I feel like to see the King's power taken from him, the Catholics persecuted, the priests hanged, the people faithful to us sent away and pursued for their lives because they served the King. As for myself, I am kept like a prisoner… with no one in the world to whom I can confide my troubles'.[20]

Although there was no going back on Charles' contrary relationship with Parliament, on his return the city of London welcomed him, the people cheering and waving along the decorated streets. The Lord Mayor held a civic banquet for the royals, Mary included and as they travelled back to Whitehall, the choir at St Paul's came out to sing to them.

But their popularity was not to last. Whilst the people had been pleased to see the Royal family, Parliament had compiled its *Grand Remonstrance* – a list of all that was seen as being wrong with Charles' government of the church and state. The king wrote a considered reply which he hoped would appease them but then he made a grave mistake. The year 1642 started with Charles' disastrous attempt to arrest five members of parliament. Arriving at the House of Commons with an armed guard of more than 300 men, he sat in the Speaker's chair and asked they be handed over to him. The men – Pym, Hampden, Holles, Strode and Haselrig – who Charles saw as leading the main opposition against him had been tipped off and escaped. Fearing retaliation, Charles and the royal family now left Whitehall and fled to Hampton Court and then Windsor but the two youngest children, Elizabeth known to her family as 'Temperance' and Henry, who had been staying at St James' Palace, had been left behind.

Charles was more concerned for his wife and this time firmly declared that she would be leaving the country with Mary to journey to Holland. He informed Parliament:

His majesty being very much pressed by the States' ambassador to send the princess his daughter immediately into Holland, and being likewise earnestly desired by his royal consort the queen to give her majesty leave to accompany her daughter thither, hath thought fit to consent to both desires, and to make this his majesty's consent and her majesty's resolution known to this parliament.[21]

Charles had approached Prince Frederick Henry of Orange for help with Parliament but he refused to get involved. At least if the prince spoke with Henrietta Maria in person she may be able to gain his support. On 12 February the king accompanied his wife and daughter to Dover to await the Dutch Admiral Van Tromp with his fifteen ship escort for Mary. Henrietta Maria had in her baggage her jewellery including a chain of pearls and a cross from her mother, much of Charles' from his ruby collar to his pearl buttons and many of the crown jewels which would be pawned to raise funds for what both herself and the king now knew would turn into civil war. Mary does not seem to have taken much with her especially nothing like the trousseau a new bride should have or like the one her mother had brought to England. By Monday 23 February conditions were suitable for sailing and Charles' farewell to his wife and daughter couldn't have been more touching. He knew he would never see his daughter again and worried also that it would be the last time he could embrace Henrietta. Henrietta lamented how circumstances 'forced me to leave the king and my children'.[22] As their boat sailed away Charles rode up and down the coastline waving his hat as his wife and daughter departed England's shores.

Storms battered their ships all the way to Helvoetsluys – a fifteen hour journey – where one of the baggage ships containing the queen's chapel plate and her entourage's luggage sank before the harbour. (In 2014 one of Countess Roxburghe's dresses was found by divers amongst other items in the recovered wreckage.) The party that travelled with them was small. Lords Goring and Arundel accompanied them whilst the Countess of Roxburghe continued in her position as Mary's governess until she handed over the reins to Catherine Stanhope and returned to look after Henry and Elizabeth. The duchess of Richmond and the Countess of Denbigh waited on the queen. Henrietta's confessor Father Philip, two Capuchin priests and her dwarf Geoffrey made up the small band of travellers.

Seasick and exhausted from their journey, the group were met by Prince William and his cousins on arrival who had planned to take them by barge to Rotterdam but Henrietta Maria could not bear another moment's travel on water and they were taken by carriage to the palace at Honselersdijk to recover. Continuing their travels, they were greeted outside The Hague by Elizabeth, Queen of Bohemia, sister to Charles I and Mary's aunt, who escorted them into the city where they were greeted by gun salute, fireworks and the ringing of church bells. Elizabeth would come to befriend Mary and be something of a surrogate mother to her in the years to come.

William's father, Prince Frederick Henry, son of William the Silent, and his mother Amelia van Solms, who was once maid of honour to the Queen of Bohemia, were waiting to greet their son's new bride. While Frederick's welcome was enthusiastic and he would in fact treat his daughter-in-law like the royalty she was, Amelia's was cooler. Perhaps jealousy played a part as Amelia could never match Mary's pedigree and the princess would soon take precedence over her. Mary felt her dislike and was uncomfortable with her mother-in-law from their first meeting. Their relationship would never be one of friendship.

Mary was entering a world vastly different from the one she had been brought up in. Holland was part of the Dutch Republic also known as the United Seven Provinces governed by the States-General. Each province was ruled by a stadtholder and decisions about governance were decided by delegates of the States-General from The Hague. Prince William was anxious that the princess should be learning their Dutch ways, language and customs and after spending two days with her mother, she was moved to new apartments. The prince may also have wanted to remove her from Henrietta Maria's influence. They all knew the state of affairs in England and did not willingly wish to accommodate the English queen who had plans of her own. This was no holiday trip for her but a chance to raise funds and supplies for her beleaguered husband and seeing Mary in safe hands, she immediately set about her task.

Mary wasn't happy. At ten years old, she found herself living in a strange country where she now had to play a new role. Baron Heenvliet was in charge of her household and his wife Catherine Stanhope would become her new governess. Catherine was an English woman who had married first Lord Henry Stanhope and later after his death had met Baron Heenvliet when he was negotiating Mary's marriage to William. They had married early in 1641 and she returned to Holland with him to take up her position as governess. She had also promised Mary's father that William would not be allowed to consummate their marriage before she was fourteen – something she would fail to do through no fault of her own.

William's father had issued orders that detailed how Mary should act, how she should behave in public and how she must always be accompanied to ensure she would never 'from negligence, inattention or want of thought' be guilty of 'any unseemly and uncivil actions'.[23] Mary felt the walls closing around her and thought her every move was spied upon.

A letter from her brother would have cheered her if it contained good news but Charles wrote of troubled times:

Most Royal Sister,
Methinks, although I cannot enjoy that former happiness which I was wont, in the fruition of your society, being barred those joys by the parting waves, yet I cannot so forget the kindness I owe unto so dear a sister, as not to write, also expecting the like salutation

from you, that thereby (although awhile dissevered) we may reciprocally understand of each other's welfare. I could heartily, and with a fervent devotion, wish your return, were it not to lessen your delights in your loyal spouse, the Prince of Orange, who, as I conceived by his last letter, was as joyful for your presence as we are sad and mourning for your absence.

My father is very much disconsolate and troubled, partly for my royal mother's and your absence, and partly for the disturbances of this kingdom.

Dear sister, we are, as much as we may, merry; and more than we would, sad, in respect we cannot alter the present distempers of these troublesome times. My father's resolution is now for York, where he intends to reside, to see the event or sequel to these bad unpropitious beginnings; whither you direct your letter. Thus much desiring your comfortable answer to these my sad lines, I rest, your loving brother.[24]

Mary would get little comfort from her mother who was busy with her own plans, selling jewels and gathering arms to send to England. Henrietta Maria had arranged to go to Amsterdam to rally support for the king but rather than see her off on her own (and not trusting her anyway), the trip turned into an Orange family state visit. They were warmly welcomed, especially the queen of England:

... there met her upon the water a most rich and costly barge, in which her majesty being entered, without help of oars or sails, she was conveyed into the city by divers living swans, which were fastened to the foresaid barge; and as she passed along, was entertained with divers triumphs upon the water. Likewise when she landed, as she passed the streets, divers pageants and other shows did present themselves unto her, which, for cost and magnificence, the like was never seen in Holland before.[25]

Unfortunately a death in the Orange family cut their stay short and on returning to The Hague, Prince William made preparations to join his army, leaving on 27 May. He asked Mary to join him later to inspect the troops and on 1 June the princess and her mother visited the camp at Voorneschantz to witness a military display and mock fight. Leaving her husband, Mary was welcomed in Utrecht and Leiden on their return journey to The Hague. It was to be a long, boring summer for the princess, forever under the watchful eye of Johan van der Kerckhove, Baron Heenvliet, with her husband away and her mother, once back in her own apartments, busy raising support for Charles I and the Royalist cause. Henrietta Maria mourned the death of her mother in July but nothing could stop her from organising money, guns and ammunition for the king. Even when Charles complained it was not enough she curtly responded 'If everyone had done their duty as I have, you would not be reduced to the condition you are now in'.[26]

The English civil war officially started on 22 August when Charles raised his royal standard over Nottingham. That it fell down in the rain could only be seen as a bad omen and the start of prolonged hostilities that were to last nine years. Mary was safely away from the bloodshed that would follow but her sister Elizabeth was now in Parliamentary control. The princess and her brother Henry remained under watch at St James' Palace. In October it was decided they should be moved to Lord Cottington's house, further away from the city centre, to escape the plague that once more was ravaging the city but Elizabeth was unwell and was given leave to stay at St James' – for the time being. The once solid Stuarts were now torn apart, never to be together as a family again.

Chapter Two

From England to France

1643–1647

Civil war would seriously affect families across England in the years to come. Divided in their loyalties, fathers, brothers, uncles and sons would fight for the Royalists or the Parliamentarians – often against one another. The first major battle at Edge Hill on 23 October 1642 had been indecisive and Charles I's reign was in turmoil, his family split asunder. His two older sons, Charles and James, were safe with him and his queen was now on her way back from Holland which was some consolation as he had feared he may never see her again but out of his two surviving daughters, one was living unhappily in Holland and little Elizabeth was in captivity with her younger brother, Henry.

In the spring of 1643 the Commons ordered an investigation into the household at St James' Palace primarily to root out any Catholics and those not loyal to Parliament. The seven-year-old Elizabeth worried about any changes to her living arrangements wrote a letter to the lords and peers in Parliament which she gave to the Earl of Pembroke to deliver.

My Lords, I account myself very miserable that I must have my servants taken from me, and strangers put to me. You promised me that you would have a care of me, and I hope you will shew it, in preventing so great a grief as this would be to me. I pray, my lords, consider of it, and give me cause to thank you, and to rest, Your loving friend, Elizabeth.[1]

The lords were unaware that the Commons had ordered such a review and so it was decided that the earls of Northumberland,

Pembroke, Manchester, and Salisbury, Lords Say and Seale, Howard, and Willoughby needed to investigate. They were not entirely happy with what they found and despite Elizabeth's letter changes were made including the returned Countess of Roxburgh being replaced by the Countess of Dorset.

Eleven servants in all were let go and those that remained had to accept an oath that included:

> ... *that I will not hinder the education of any of the king's children in the true Protestant religion, piety, or holiness of life ; but will, according to my place, calling, and duty, advance the same; and if I know that any person doth endeavour to hinder such education of any of them, I will make the same known, at least to three of the committee appointed by the two Houses of Parliament, for the regulating of the household of St. James's, whereof there shall be one lord and two commons. I do further covenant and promise, that I will no way endeavour to work or cause any misunderstanding or disaffection between any of the king's children and either House of Parliament, or any member of either house; but if I know any practice or endeavour of this kind, I will reveal the same, as aforesaid. And I do further promise, that if I receive any message or letter from Oxford, or the court, or any place where soever, that concerns the removal of the king's children, or any of them, or that may be prejudicial to the Houses of Parliament, or any one of them, or any member thereof, I will reveal the same as aforesaid. Neither will I send any letter, or give any word or message, to be sent to Oxford or elsewhere, that may be prejudicial to the king's children, or to either or both Houses of Parliament, or any member of either house. Neither will I, in my own person, repair to Oxford, or any other the king's quarters, during this war, without leave first had of the aforesaid committee, or five of them at the least.*[2]

Charles was increasingly worried about his daughter and youngest son and correspondence was sent to Parliament to enquire after their well-being. It was suggested that a swop could be arranged – the children for Parliamentary prisoners of war – but as Parliament refused to admit the children were prisoners themselves the suggestion came to nothing.

For the time being they would remain at St James', Elizabeth filling her time with her studies. A studious and bright young girl, she had been tutored since 1640 by Bathsua Makin, a woman known for her intelligence and learning. Elizabeth learnt Latin, Greek, Hebrew, French, Italian and Spanish under the care of Makin who was a firm supporter of a woman's right to education. Music, singing, dancing, writing and needlework were added to her curriculum. She loved reading and studying the Scriptures which helped to relieve the boredom of recuperation when she broke her leg in the autumn of 1643. Later investigation would show that she suffered from rickets – a weakening of the bones. By 1644 she was well enough to move to the house of Sir John Danvers – a man who would later sign her father's death warrant – in pleasant Chelsea with its Italian gardens. There is no record that she met with her mother or father during this time who were based in Oxford, a Royalist stronghold.

Henrietta Maria had attempted to return to England on 2 February 1643 but storms had forced her ships back to Scheveningen after nine tortuous days and nights of being tossed amongst the waves. After repairs she set sail again arriving at Bridlington Bay on the Yorkshire coast. During the night Parliament ships arrived and began to fire. Henrietta and her ladies were bundled out of the cottage they were staying in to hide in a ditch whilst cannon shot whistled across their heads for two hours. The captain of the Dutch vessels ordered the Parliamentarians to stop or he would retaliate. When firing ceased Henrietta gave orders for her treasured ammunition to be loaded into carts for their onward journey on to York. It was a slow ride during which Henrietta heard that Parliament had impeached her for high treason. Moving on to Newark she wrote to Charles 'I carry with me three thousand foot, thirty companies of horse and dragoons, six pieces of cannon and two mortars'.[3] Nothing was going to dissuade 'her she-majesty and extremely diligent generalissima'[4] from reaching the king at Oxford and providing him with men and ammunition for the Royalist cause.

Their reunion was an emotional one and before long Henrietta Maria was pregnant with her ninth child and into this war torn country, the king's last daughter would be born. The queen was feeling extremely unwell in the end stages of her pregnancy and Oxford was no place for her confinement. Charles accompanied her as far as Abingdon where after a tearful farewell she left him to travel south, originally considering Bristol as a safe haven but eventually arriving in Exeter, another Royalist stronghold under the command of Sir John Berkeley, on 1 May 1644. Henrietta Maria painfully made her way to Bedford House owned by the Russell family and there prepared for the birth of her last child.

Charles I was extremely worried about the health of his wife and wrote to his trusted doctor, Thomas Mayerne, 'Mayerne, for love of me, go to my wife'.[5] The doctor was in London and suffering ill health himself when he received a further letter from Henrietta in which she wrote 'retaining in my memory the care you have ever taken of me in my utmost need, it makes me believe that if you can, you will come...'[6] He arrived in Exeter on 28 May. Madame Peronne, a French midwife, who had attended Henrietta's sister-in-law Anne of Austria, the queen mother of France and Henrietta's previous births, was sent to aid her delivery and came bearing gifts of baby clothes, money and an invitation to return to France once she was recovered. Although Spanish, Anne was of Hapsburg descent, and was a staunch supporter of her sister-in-law and would do everything in her power to help her.

Henrietta Maria was surrounded by loyal and trusted servants but she feared for her life. She wrote to Charles:

The weak state in which I am, caused by the cruel pains I have suffered since I left you, which have been too severe to be experienced or understood by any but those who have suffered them, makes me believe that it is time to think of another world... Let it not trouble you, I beg. You know well that from my last confinement, I have reason to fear and also to hope. By preparing for the worst, we are never taken by surprise and good fortune appears so much the better. Adieu, my dear heart. I hope before I leave you, to see you once again in the position in which you ought to be...[7]

On 16 June the queen gave birth to her daughter also named Henrietta who would later have the name Anne added to hers in gratitude for the help Anne of Austria had given. The queen had a painful birth. She was suffering from rheumatic fever and was 'in a state of extreme weakness and suffering'[8] but she had no time to recuperate. Parliamentary troops were moving towards Exeter and Henrietta feared she would be captured. She asked for safe conduct to move to Bath but Robert Devereux, 3rd Earl of Essex, in charge of the besieging troops swore that if she were to go anywhere it would be to London to answer for her actions in sustaining the war. The Commons determined she was answerable to their laws especially since she had never been crowned. Her enemies saw her as a bargaining tool and if captured they could use her to sway Charles to their demands. She had no intention of making her husband's position more difficult than it already was. If she could reach France she would be safe and could rally support for Charles' cause from afar as she had once done in Holland. Making her plans she wrote touchingly to her husband:

I will show you by this last action that there is nothing that lies so near my heart as your safety. My life is but a small thing compared with that. For in the present state of affairs your condition would be in great peril if you came to my relief, and I know that your affection would make you risk all for my sake. And so I prefer to risk this miserable life of mine, a thing worthless enough in itself, saving in as far as it is precious to you. My dear heart, farewell. The most unhappy creature in the world who can no longer hold a pen.[9]

At just two weeks old, she left her daughter 'a small and delicate babe'[10] in the care of Lady Anne Dalkeith, wife of Robert Douglas, Lord Dalkeith, eldest son of the Earl of Morton and daughter of Sir Edward Villiers, half-brother to the Duke of Buckingham together with Sir John Berkeley, governor of Exeter. They would guard her with their lives as her mother escaped the town.

Henrietta Maria was still unwell, described as 'worn and pitiful'[11] and had to be carried in a litter towards the coast, hiding from Parliamentary soldiers whenever they crossed their paths listening to boasts 'that they would carry the head of Henrietta to London as they should receive from the parliament a reward for it of 50,000 crowns'.[12] Making her way to Falmouth she was welcomed by John Arundel at Pendennis Castle, a Royalist stronghold and one of the coastal forts originally built in the reign of Henry VIII overlooking the English Channel. Here she got word that her daughter was unwell, suffering convulsions, and she sent her doctor Sir John Hinton (sometimes named as Winton) back to the baby Henrietta.

As the little one struggled to survive, albeit in the loving care of Lady Dalkeith, her mother sailed for France on 14 July on a Flemish ship. It was not to be an easy voyage. Parliamentary ships seeing the queen fleeing to safety chased after them firing their cannons. Henrietta Maria demanded that the captain of her vessel sink them rather than be taken by her enemies but fortunately as the wind picked up, the Flemish ship surged forward and the arrival of French ships deterred the English from continuing their pursuit. The wind that had aided them then turned to gale force as a storm assailed their vessel and drove them on to rocks near Brest. Her son, Charles, in later years would joke with his sister about 'Mam's bad fortune at sea'.[13] Henrietta Maria and her companions had to scramble over rocks, soaked and exhausted, until they reached the safety of a cluster of fishermen's huts. The local villagers gave the queen and her companions shelter and food and as soon as Anne of Austria heard of Henrietta Maria's predicament she sent carriages and doctors to bring her to Paris and the royal court. But Henrietta's health was compromised. She had been unwell for weeks now and this further journey had made her worse. The doctors recommended that she go to Bourbon to take the waters first and it would be months before she was well enough to join the French court. But at least she was now safe, unlike those she had left behind in England.

Lady Dalkeith was becoming increasingly worried about remaining in Exeter with her precious charge. Still she had her job to do and whilst there she organised for Henrietta to be baptised in the cathedral on 21 July by Dr Lawrence Burnell, the Dean of Exeter, with herself, Lady Poulett and Sir John Berkeley as sponsors.

Charles I was earnestly worrying about his wife and children but his situation was precarious. He still had hope his reign would be restored soon and without much further bloodshed. His Royalist commander and nephew Prince Rupert of the Rhine had some success in skirmishes at Stockport and Bolton but the Battle of Marston Moor on 2 July had been a Parliamentary victory. There would be no peaceful solution as yet to the civil war that continued to tear England apart. Anxious for news of his family, Charles arrived in Exeter on 26 July accompanied by his eldest son the Prince of Wales to find his queen had fled but his daughter was in loving care. He missed his indomitable wife lamenting 'Although I have much cause to be troubled by my wife's departure from me and out of my dominions, yet not her absence so much as the scandal of that necessity which drives her away doth afflict me, that she should be compelled by my own subjects and those pretending to be Protestants to withdraw for her safety...'[14] Charles was overcome with emotion as he held his youngest child in his arms, his tears dripping on the innocent baby born at such a tumultuous time. Satisfied she was well looked after and in no immediate danger, Charles could only stay one night before he left her to join his troops, chasing the Earl of Essex into Cornwall, but returned to her again for a month in September. The excise duties of the town were assigned to support Henrietta Anne's household and he employed Dr Thomas Fuller as her chaplain, who took to his duties rigorously composing pamphlets of instruction to be of use to his charge as she grew up. One of which, *Good Thoughts in Bad Times*, he had especially bound in blue morocco cloth embossed with a coronet which was presented to the baby Henrietta and remained with her throughout her life. But King Charles could not stay any longer and this time he made his farewell to his daughter not knowing that this would be the last time they would ever meet.

One daughter who was desperate to see her father was under another man's control. On 13 March 1645 it was reported 'The lords were pleased this day to make the noble Earl of Northumberland governor, and his lady governess, of His Majesty's children now at Whitehall'.[15] Algernon Percy, the 10th Earl of Northumberland, who had once been Charles I's Lord High Admiral, was paid £3000 a year with an extra £9500 for Elizabeth and Henry's expenses. He had every intention of making sure they were well looked after and moved them to Syon House, a former Bridgettine abbey, further outside of London. But within weeks their expenses were cut to £5000 a year and the earl was ordered to bring them back to the city though he could choose where from Whitehall, Somerset House or St. James' and 'take tapestries, bedding, plate, furniture, &c. from the royal stores, as he thought fitting, for their use'.[16] So back to St James' the children travelled.

Elizabeth was allowed to write to Mary 'Dear Sister, I am glad of so fit an opportunity to present my love to you. I intended to have sent you some venison, but being prevented at this time, I hope I shall have it ready to entertain you at The Hague, when you return'.[17] It is not known whether Mary wrote in reply. Her situation in Holland had not improved. Another wedding ceremony had been performed in 1643 when she was twelve and she now had more of a role to play in state, giving audiences and attending functions. But she did not take to these easily and her husband, who she had grown closer to, was often away campaigning leaving her to the mercy of her mother-in-law who still insisted that she was more important than a young princess.

In England on 14 June 1645 the Parliamentarians won a decisive victory at the Battle of Naseby. Charles' bid to remain in control of his country was slipping through his fingers. In August the Prince of Wales managed to visit his sister Henrietta for a month but by the winter Exeter was in a state of siege. Lady Dalkeith had hoped to escape to Cornwall but once more the town was surrounded and although dangerous to stay, it was too dangerous to leave. Dalkeith had nothing but the baby Henrietta's welfare at heart but from the safety of her comfortable apartment in France, Henrietta Maria was berating her faithful servant for delaying in taking her daughter to safety. Charles' chancellor Sir Edward Hyde, Earl of Clarendon wrote to Lord Jermyn, the queen mother's chief advisor in France, in her defence.

I think it will break her heart when she hears of the Queen's displeasure; which pardon me for saying, is with much severity conceived against her... the governess is as faultless in the business as you are, and has been as punctual as solicitous, and as impatient to obey the Queen's directions, as she could be to save her soul. She could not act her part without assistance; and what assistance could she have? How could she have left Exeter, and whither have gone?[18]

Hyde continued to relay the state of affairs in Exeter and the uproar caused over the rumours that the Prince of Wales would be taken to France.

Was this the time to remove the Princess? Had it been done, all security for the prince's safety would have passed away. The governess would have procured a pass to bring the princess to Cornwall, had not the letters been taken at Dartwell, by which the designs of transporting her transpired. You now have the whole story, and may conclude the governess could as easily have beaten Fairfax, as prevented being shut up in Exeter, from whence I hope she will yet get safely with her charge, to whom I am confident she hath omitted no part of her duty.[19]

Lady Dalkeith was fervently trying to find a way to get baby Henrietta to safety but it wasn't until 13 April 1646 that the Agreement of Exeter, the terms of surrender, were finally signed. These included instructions concerning the Princess. She was to stay in Exeter or move within twenty days. Lady Dalkeith immediately wrote to the king for his orders. As soon as she received a reply she sent a letter to Sir Thomas Fairfax, general of the Parliamentary troops. Saying:

... I have his Majesty's allowance to remain with the Princess for some time about London, in any of his Majesty's houses. I have judged Richmond the fittest. This bearer will inform you of those particulars concerning the settlement of the Princess in that place, wherein I conceive your assistance and recommendation to the parliament to be necessary, which his Majesty will acknowledge as a service and I as an obligation...[20]

Instead of Richmond, Sir John Berkeley was allowed to escort

Lady Dalkeith and Henrietta Anne to Oatlands in Surrey. There her household was organised but with Dalkeith's own money. The excise duties they had received in Exeter were no longer forthcoming and letters to Parliament asking for financial assistance went unheeded. In fact Parliament had decided that Lady Dalkeith should disband Henrietta's household and no longer look after the princess. She should join her elder brother Henry and sister Elizabeth at St James' Palace where she would be more closely under their supervision. Horrified the lady wrote to the Speaker of the House of Commons imploring them to let her remain with her charge. When she received no reply she began to make plans to flee with the youngest Stuart child.

Things had not being going well for Charles I and his eldest son. The Prince of Wales had escaped to the Scilly Isles in March and on 27 April Charles I left Oxford and surrendered to the Scots as they besieged Newark. Prince Rupert of the Rhine had been left in charge of Oxford but when the Parliamentary troops surrounded the town he was forced to surrender and on 24 June he led 2000 men from the besieged Royalist stronghold. The terms of surrender stated that Rupert could stay in England for six months but he was not to stay within twenty miles of London. After this period he must go overseas. But General Fairfax allowed him to go to Oatlands and because it was close to London Parliament then declared that he had 'broken the articles agreed upon to repair to the seaside within ten days, and forthwith to depart the kingdom'.[21]

A defeated Prince Rupert told Lady Dalkeith of his arrangements to leave for France in July and must have helped in working out the details of their own escape. Although they could not travel together Lady Dalkeith was inspired to take Henrietta Anne to her mother at the chateau at Saint-Germain-en-Laye, the queen's childhood home, west of Paris. It was becoming too dangerous for the young Stuart princess to remain in England. Her brother James had been sent to join Elizabeth and Henry at

St James' Palace whereas Charles, Prince of Wales, had moved on to Jersey in April and answering his mother's entreaties would arrive in Paris in June.

Lady Dalkeith was ready to make her move. She dressed herself, a French valet to act as her husband and the princess as beggars, to go unnoticed. Henrietta Anne was disguised as a boy and referred to as Pierre as they set out on foot from Oatlands heading for Dover. The little girl frequently remonstrated that she was in fact a princess and that those clothes really weren't hers. Fortunately no one paid them any attention as Lady Dalkeith carried Henrietta nearly a hundred miles closely followed by Sir John Berkeley at a distance to ensure their safety. With great relief they boarded a French ship to sail to Calais. When Henrietta Maria heard of her daughter's arrival she immediately sent carriages to the port to convey them to Saint-Germain and on her arrival 'Oh the transports of joy, Oh the excessive consolation to the heart of the Queen. She embraced, she hugged and kissed again and again the royal infant'.[22]

Lady Dalkeith was worn out by her exertions and as soon as she had safely delivered her charge to her mother she succumbed to illness unaware that she had become the heroine of the hour and the talk of the court for such a daring flight from danger. Back in England, Parliament were unaware of her escape for three days after their departure. Although the servants at Oatlands had been alarmed to find them missing, Lady Dalkeith sent them a letter in which she asked they delay in informing the authorities:

Gentlewomen, You are witness with what patience I have expected the pleasure of Parliament. I have found it impossible to obtain any justice to Her Highness or favour to myself, or any of you. I was no longer able to keep her, which was the cause I have been forced to take this upon me… It will be a great mark of your faithfulness and kindness to your mistress, to conceal her being gone as long as you can...[23]

It appears that not only were the servants she left behind faithful but that there had been others that aided their escape. Years later two petitions were presented to Charles II. One from an Elinor Dyke was for unpaid wages for her years of service in Exeter and also the loss of her house and belongings when she attended the princess into France. The other from Thomas Lambert and his wife Mary also asks for financial aid due to 'their diligence in convoying the Princess Henrietta, from her barbarous enemies to the queen mother in France'.[24]

Father Cyprien de Gamache who recorded Henrietta Anne's arrival in his diary and would later feature in the princess's life as teacher and spiritual guide wrote that her mother regarded

> ... *the princess as a child of blessing (une enfant de benediction). She resolved with the grace of God, to have her instructed in the Catholic and Roman religion, and to use all her efforts to obtain the consent of the King her husband.*[25]

Back when Lady Dalkeith had arranged the princess's christening she had done so at Charles I's behest in an Anglican ceremony the same way all the queen's children had been christened but Henrietta Maria saw her daughter as her special blessing. Now in France, a Catholic country, it made sense to raise her in the same religion. Even though it may anger the king in England, it pleased the queen mother and regent of France. Henrietta was at the mercy of her sister-in-law Anne who thankfully was extremely supportive of her. Ruling in her son Louis XIV's stead with her chief minister Cardinal Mazarin, Anne made sure the English exiles were well looked after.

The princess Henrietta Anne settled into life with her mother and brother Charles in apartments that had been allocated to them at the royal palace of the Louvre in the centre of Paris.

The exiled queen of England was allowed a generous pension of 30,000 livres a month but her expenses were high. She kept a large household which was costly to maintain and also supported Royalists who fled to join her as well as sending money to her husband.

Summer was spent with the court at the magnificent chateau at Fontainebleau where Louis XIV enjoyed hunting but they were also allowed the use of the palace of Saint-Germain as they wished for their country residence. For now it was important for Charles to meet his French relatives and make solid connections to cement the relationship between the Stuarts of England and France. Henrietta Maria thought that might be with an advantageous marriage of Charles to her niece Anna Marie Louise d'Orleans, known as La Grande Mademoiselle, and heiress to a fortune, but neither were impressed with Henrietta's matchmaking. La Grande Mademoiselle wrote of Charles as being 'rather tall for his age, a fine head, black hair, a brown complexion and passably agreeable in person'. So not bad looking then but 'what was extremely inconvenient, was that he neither spoke nor understood a word of French'.[26] At several fetes and banquets Henrietta convinced her son to pay her niece much attention but La Grande Mademoiselle had other ideas about her love life 'the Queen of England noticed that I looked at her son somewhat disdainfully. When she learned the cause of it she reproached me and said that my head was full of nothing but the Emperor. I defended myself as well as I could, but my face disguised my sentiments so poorly that one had only to look at me to discover them'.[27] It was fine by Charles. He had no intention of marrying yet nor would he let his mother dictate to whom when he did.

It was a trying end to the year but Henrietta Maria still had hope that her husband might come to an arrangement with his enemies. Charles had written to Mary asking for a warship which she duly sent in November 1646. The thirty-four gun ship carved with images of Mary and William awaited the king but although he plotted to escape he was too heavily guarded. In January 1647 the Scots sold Charles I to Parliament for £400,000. He had gone from one form of custody to another and Henrietta Maria began to truly despair for her husband as he was transferred under guard to Holdenby House. She received the last letter from him that would come for some time which started 'Deare Hart, I must tell thee that now I am declared what I have really beene ever since I came to this army, which is a prisoner'.[28]

In April Cromwell's New Model Army took charge of the king and after being moved around the country over the next few months he was finally settled at Hampton Court Palace. At least here he was allowed to see his children James, Henry and Elizabeth who were staying at nearby Syon House up river. Later in the summer, they were allowed to spend two days with their father at Caversham and en route stopped at the Greyhound Inn where Elizabeth met General Fairfax, commander of the Parliamentary forces. She thanked him for the chance to see the king and 'for the high happiness she now enjoyed in the sight of her dear father, which she knew was obtained only by his industry and management'.[29] The little princess was so charming the general asked for permission to kiss her hand.

Parliament did not really know what to do with these Stuart children moving them from one place to the other for their safety. When the army took possession of London, they were moved from St James' back to Syon House, the Earl of Northumberland's seat, and from there were allowed several visits to their father at Hampton Court throughout August and September. In October the children were ready to move back into London for the winter but Charles asked they be allowed to stay with him for the weekend first. He wrote to Elizabeth 'it is not through forgetfulness, or any want of kindness, that I have not all this time sent for you, but for such reasons as is fitter for you to imagine, which you may easily do, than me to write; but now I hope to see you upon Friday or Saturday next'.[30] The weekend was only marred by Elizabeth's complaint that she could not sleep due to the soldiers tramping up and down. Their captain had already ordered them to tread quietly around the children but when Charles remonstrated with him, he suggested he could send his guards further off as long as the king promised he would not try to escape. Charles agreed for the sake of his children but just weeks later he fled to the Isle of Wight with a notion that from there he might take ship. He believed the governor of the island Robert Hammond to be loyal but he was soon incarcerated in Carisbrooke Castle. If his escape had gone to plan he would have joined his family in France.

Henrietta Maria was devastated at the news of her husband's incarceration. She did not know how to help him. Could she find support in Ireland and what of those in France who had promised their support? She sent an envoy to the Marquis of Ormonde, Charles I's Lord Lieutenant, in Dublin but he was forced to relinquish control of his 3000 Royalist troops to Parliament and was in fear of his own arrest. She turned to those in France but Cardinal Mazarin, Anne of Austria's advisor, wished their country to remain neutral. Her only comfort was in her children; three were still in England, one in Holland, but for now she had control of Charles, Prince of Wales and heir to the English throne, and of course, her 'bebe de benediction', Princess Henrietta Anne.

Charles I

Chapter Three

Tragic Times

1648–1653

The twelve-year-old Elizabeth had little in her life to comfort her. Occasionally she received letters from her father and wrote to him often uncertain of whether he would receive them. In February she wrote 'the greatest terrestrial joy that can be to me, is to hear that you are in health and prosperity, and nothing hath been such a terror to me as that I have not heard from you so frequently as formerly'.[1] At least it had been a joy to have her older brother James with her for a time but she knew he would have to leave England soon for his own safety.

James, Duke of York, was second in line to the throne and as such his father was urging him to escape abroad. Parliament found his secret correspondence with the king detailing a planned attempt and threatened with the Tower, James responded:

> I understand that there was a Letter of mine intercepted, going to the King; which, I confess, was a Fault: And therefore I desire you to let the House know, that I will engage my Honour and Faith, never to engage myself any more in such Businesses.[2]

But of course he was still looking for a way out as Elizabeth knew. As his mother and sister before him, James had to be inventive in order to escape Parliament's grasp. Every evening he played hide and seek with his younger siblings and was so good at hiding, he sometimes did not appear for half an hour or more. It set the scene for his disappearance and bought him time. On 20 April, after such a game he managed to slip through the gardens at St James's Palace and was met by Colonel Bampfield who took him to a safe house near London Bridge. There the colonel's mistress, Anne Murray, had clothes ready to disguise James as a young gentlewoman. She recalled in her memoirs the reaction of the tailor when given the duke's measurements 'he considered it a long time and said he had many many such gowns and suits, but he had never made any to such a person in his life. I thought he was in the right; but his meaning was, he had never seen any woman of so low stature have so big a waist. However, he made it exactly fit as if he had taken the measure himself. It was a mixed mohair of a light hair colour and black, and the under petticoat was scarlet'.[3] Looking the part but fiddling with his garter and stockings, James was found out by the barge man employed to take him down river but no alarm was raised and the duke boarded a Dutch ship which immediately sailed for Flushing.

James was reunited with his sister Mary at The Hague, who immediately ordered tailors to make him a new set of clothes. He later remembered 'the affectionateness of which meeting I cannot express'.[4] Mary's father-in-law had died the previous year making William stadtholder of Holland, Zeeland, Utrecht, Guelders and Overijssel and now Mary and William were in a position to offer her brothers the support they needed in exile.

Mary wanted French help to restore her father and Charles had been waiting at Calais for permission to leave France but the French Chief Minister, Cardinal Mazarin refused to let him go, sticking to his neutrality until June, when the turmoil that was brewing in his own country became more important than the whereabouts of the Prince of Wales and Mary's desires. Charles still had everything to aim for. Although he was detained, his father had secretly signed an agreement with the Scots to establish Presbyterianism in England and to include their representatives in his Privy Council in return for his restoration to the throne. Charles planned to join the Scottish army to free the king. When he heard that ships loyal to the Stuarts had docked in Helvoetsluys, he travelled to Holland where he met up with his siblings. It was a grand reunion with Mary, James and their cousins Rupert, Maurice and Philip. Charles' detour to Holland to meet with the Royalist sailors meant that by the time he reached Scotland, he was too late to reach the troops before they were defeated at the Battle of Preston by Oliver Cromwell and his New Model Army. This last attempt to save his father failed miserably. Queen Henrietta Maria had gone to the convent in Faubourg Saint-Jacques to pray for Charles' success but her prayers were unanswered and her son dejectedly returned to Holland.

As troubled by civil war as England was, France had its own uprising to contend with. Whilst the French court had decamped to Saint-Germain to avoid the riots in Paris known as the War of the Fronde, Henrietta Maria had decided to stay at the Louvre with her daughter. Here she felt she would receive any correspondence from her husband all the quicker as she waited anxiously for news. She had come from a war torn country and to live in the centre of another in turmoil did not phase her but without the support of the court and especially Queen Anne her situation was becoming dire. Madame de Motteville visited them on 14 July 1648 and saw how poor they had become when 'the Queen showed her a little gold cup, out of which she drank, and told her that this was the only coin which she possessed in the world'.[5]

They would receive no help from those at the French court who were torn apart by the involvement of some of their own especially Louis XIV's uncle, Gaston and his daughter, Mademoiselle de Montpensier, La Grande Mademoiselle. The self-imposed exile of the French court reduced their circumstances to the point where 'those who had beds had no hangings, and those who had hangings were without clothes'.[6] Anne of Austria admitted there was no money, food or clothes for themselves let alone their dependants.

With no money and provisions running low, little Henrietta Anne spent her days hidden in the once sumptuous Louvre, avoiding yet another siege, looked after by Lady Dalkeith as their situation worsened. In January 1649, Cardinal Retz found them freezing and without food. The Stuart princess was tucked up in bed in an effort to keep warm. Retz could not believe how bad their situation had become stating 'posterity will hardly believe that a Queen of England and granddaughter of Henri Quatre and her daughter wanted firewood in this month of January'.[7] He immediately arranged for fuel and food to be brought to them as well as the resumption of their allowance.

The Queen of England brought so low wanted nothing but to be allowed to travel to England to see her husband. She sent letters to Parliament but received no reply. She was seen as being guilty of high treason and did not warrant a favourable response. Unknown to Henrietta Maria and her daughter, Charles I's days were numbered.

However Elizabeth, described by the French ambassador as a 'budding young beauty',[8] was writing to her father and knew all was not well. Probably urged on by Charles, she wrote to Parliament that she be allowed to go to her sister in Holland. How fantastic it would be if she could meet with Charles, James and Mary. She might even then get to go to France and be reunited with her mother but alas she also did not receive a reply.

After two unsuccessful escape attempts Charles I was moved from Carisbrooke Castle on 6 September 1648 and stayed in Newport on the island whilst negotiations were underway. After their failure he was transferred to Hurst Castle in Hampshire and then to Windsor Castle and on to London. It had been decided he should be charged with high treason. Charles I's trial was conducted at by the High Court of Justice at Westminster Hall from 20th to 27th January. Watched by over 5000 people Charles declared

> ... I would know by what authority I was brought from thence [the Isle of Wight], and carried from place to place, and I know not what: and when I know what lawful authority, I should answer. Remember, I am your King, your lawful King... I have a trust committed to me

by God, by old and lawful descent; I will not betray it, to answer you a new unlawful authority...[9]

But nothing he could say now would change his fate. The verdict 'that the said Charles Stuart as a Tyrant, Traitor, Murderer and Public Enemy shall be put to death by the severing his head from his body'[10] was read out on the 27th. Elizabeth and Henry, the two children still under Parliament's control, were allowed to see him two days later. Elizabeth recalled:

He wished me not to grieve and torment myself for him, for that it would be a glorious death that he should die, it being for the laws and liberties of this land, and for maintaining the true Protestant religion ... he told me he had forgiven all his enemies, and hoped God would forgive them also, and commanded us, and all the rest of my brothers and sisters to forgive them. He bid me tell my mother that his thoughts had never strayed from her, and that his love should be the same to the last. Withal he commanded me and my brother to be obedient to her, and bid me send his blessing to the rest of my brothers and sisters, with commendation to all his friends.[11]

Charles then shared an embrace with Henry and warned him he must not be a king whilst his brothers still lived. He gave them both pieces of his jewellery and kissed them before turning to leave the room but Elizabeth was so upset she cried and cried until her father came back for a final embrace. He was executed the next day at Whitehall.

Elizabeth and Henry were devastated by their father's death and must have wondered what would happen to them now. Dutch envoys from their sister Mary visited them and noted that only the children wore black, the rest of the household did not appear to be mourning. Elizabeth would not be well for months to come, traumatised by her father's death her ill health exacerbated and once again she asked to be allowed to go to her sister in Holland but again her request was refused. She was destined to stay in England – never to meet her family again.

The Earl of Northumberland, even though a Parliamentarian, was shocked that recent events had culminated in the killing of a king. He no longer felt he could manage the safety of the Stuart children and he was also in debt for their care. He wrote to the Council of State:

> I have for some months past been put to maintain the Duke of Gloucester and his sister out of my own purse; and for want of those allowances which I should have received by appointment of parliament, have run myself so far out of money that I am altogether destitute of means to provide longer for them, or indeed, for my own poor family unless I may have what is owing to me…The maintaining and safe-keeping of these children being matters of state, I knew not where to apply myself for directions as unto this council; humbly desiring that you may be pleased to consider how they may otherwise be disposed of.[12]

He would receive a payment for what he was owed and the children were now assigned to Sir Edward Harrington and his wife but after Harrington's son pleaded they were too old and in too poor health to take on the responsibility of Elizabeth and Henry. Northumberland suggested his sister, the Countess of Leicester 'I am confident you believe she will as much intend the good education of the children as any person that can be employed about them, and for her good affections to the Parliament, I think none that know anything of her will doubt them'.[13]

They were moved from Syon to Penshurst Place in Kent to the home of Robert Sidney, 3rd Earl of Leicester and his wife Dorothy with a promise of £3000 a year for their keep. Dorothy took the children under her wing and provided a tutor, Richard Lovell, to continue their education. She had several children of her own and for the first time in years Elizabeth and Henry became part of a family with other children to play with. Dorothy was under strict orders not to treat them as royalty but she furnished their rooms with furniture from Whitehall and allowed them to eat at a separate table with their own servants to wait on them. The fourteen-year-old Elizabeth would thrive under her care and her health would improve over the coming months.

Only the earl had any complaints but was happy to take a share of their allowance.

The parliament placed the Duke of Gloucester and the princess Elizabeth with my wife, allowing for them £3,000 a year, which was a great accession of means to my wife in proportion to the charge of these two children and ten or eleven servants; and considering my expenses in fuel, washing and household stuff etc, also that I should have less liberty in my own house than I had, and be obliged in attendance which would be troublesome to me, I thought it very reasonable to abate a great part of that £700 a year, and so from midsummer 1649, I resolved to take off £400 a year – this caused a great storm in the house but I persisted in it.[14]

The news of Charles I's death did not reach France until February and no one wanted to be the one to tell the king's wife. It was left to Lord Jermyn to break the sad and tragic news that reverberated across Europe. Henrietta Maria remained quiet, frozen by shock until her daughter, chatting away as a five-year-old will, shook the queen from her reverie. In no way could she believe that Parliament had actually executed their anointed king. It was all she could do to hand Henrietta Anne over to Lady Dalkeith whilst she retired to the convent at Faubourg Saint-Jacques, shutting herself away from the world, to grieve 'a king, a husband, and a friend, whose loss she could never sufficiently mourn'.[15]

Mary had been given the news by her husband who had been hailed by a boat carrying the sad tidings whilst out sailing. She sent a messenger to Charles who was staying with her at the time 'living a private life while awaiting a wind more favourable to his affairs'.[16] The princess was too upset to tell him the news herself and she too took time out from the world at a retreat in Spa.

Soon Parliament sent an English envoy to The Hague in the form of Dr Dorislaus. Mary was appalled that one of the men who had sat at her father's trial should have the temerity to come anywhere near her. Others must have felt the same as the ambassador was murdered the day after his arrival. William, it was said, turned a blind eye to his murderers but Charles was asked to leave to avoid further tensions rising and Mary and her husband accompanied him to new lodgings in Breda.

William's role as stadtholder was not a smooth one. He had been forced to sign the Treaty of Münster in 1648 – a declaration of peace with Spain. It was something his father had worked towards but William felt the only way the Netherlands would be free of the Spanish was by war. His mother disagreed with him, even though she had once been rumoured to be in the pay of Spain, and urged him to peace. The States wanted him to disband his troops but he refused. There were conflicting opinions and the town of Amsterdam refused to concur and allow William entry. He despatched Count William of Nassau to persuade Bickers, the burgomaster, otherwise and ordered the arrest of six men who opposed him. When Nassau failed, William rode out at the head of an army to take the town but Amsterdam would not easily fall and could open sluice gates that would flood the surrounding area and William's men. Diplomacy won the day with Bickers being dismissed and William conceding to liberate his prisoners. But it left a nasty taste in the mouths of the people and someone they could blame was Mary. She, they felt, was behind William's aggressive policies. Even with her husband as stadtholder Mary's life would not be easy.

Her sister, Princess Henrietta Anne, stayed in the Louvre with her governess and Father Cyprien Gamache, her mother's long-serving Capuchin priest. The first War of the Fronde was over by March and they could look to more peaceful times – at least until renewed hostilities began again the following year. As with her mother, religion played an important part in Henrietta Anne's life even at a young age and it provided her solace while her mother was away. Father Cyprien was responsible for Henrietta Anne's religious education and gives us one of the first insights into the young princess's life. He would later write:

> ... the Queen thought it necessary to make known, not only to France, but to all the neighbouring states, that Madame her daughter was brought up in the profession of the Catholic, Apostolic and Roman church. For this purpose she commanded me to write, print and publish the Christian instructions which I had given to the young princess. This command, and the order of my superiors, obliged me to give to the world 'Les Exercises d'une Ame Royale', containing the duties which every Christian owes to God, to the Saints, to his neighbour, and to himself, with the instructions and practices of the employments usual on working days and on holidays. These exercises, contained in three volumes, 8vo., were preceded by another small book, which explains the obligations of baptisms. All these books, being published and distributed, made known what the Queen desired, namely, that Madame Henriette, her daughter, was educated in the Catholic religion.[17]

He also relates her attempts to sway Lady Dalkeith:

> I recollect that one day, the Queen her mother, seeing her with pleasure so warm in the cause of religion, said to her 'My dear, as you have so much zeal, why do you not convert your governante?' 'Madam', answered the Princess, 'I do as much as I can in that way'. 'And what is that', rejoined the Queen. 'Madam', answered the Princess, in her infantine innocence, 'I embrace my governante, I kiss her, I say to her

"Lady Morton, be converted, be a catholic, you must be a catholic to be saved. Father Cyprien tells me so very often; you have heard him as well as I, be a good lady, and I will love you dearly".[18]

Henrietta Anne would always be devoted to her religion and Lady Dalkeith but her governess would not be convinced to convert. The princess knew no other religious teaching and in France it was normal to be Catholic. Her brother Charles however was appalled that his mother had managed to ignore her husband's wishes on the matter of Henrietta's religion. It was imperative for the Prince of Wales to uphold the Protestant faith as his father had done. He knew England would not accept him as a Catholic king should he be restored.

Although England declared itself a republic in March, the Scots had proclaimed Charles as king in February and he began to negotiate with Scottish Parliament for his return. Returning to Jersey in September, he decided to travel to Ireland and rally the Royalist troops there but Cromwell's catastrophic invasion of the Emerald Isle stopped his plans. By May 1650 he was sailing for Scotland to join his supporters.

There was further tragedy in September when the now dowager-queen Henrietta Maria heard the news that her daughter Elizabeth had died. In August the Countess of Leicester received a visit from William Lenthall, Speaker of the House. He was appalled to see Elizabeth and Henry eating separately and being deferred to when he had given strict instructions for them to be treated as just ordinary household members. Not long after an order was given for their removal.

Elizabeth and Henry were moved to Carisbrooke Castle on the Isle of Wight under the care of Governor Anthony Mildmay. Whilst playing bowls outside they had been caught in a torrential downpour and Elizabeth came down with a fever. The local physician Dr Bignall was called but as she worsened a dispatch was sent to the royal doctor Mayerne who was too ill to come himself but sent another in his stead with pertinent remedies. They arrived too late.

Elizabeth died just as Parliament finally agreed she could be sent to live with her sister in The Hague. She had probably been afflicted with tuberculosis for some time when this final illness finished her suffering. Her mother Henrietta Maria believed she died 'at finding herself taken to the same castle where the king her father had been kept prisoner, and in a place where she had no assistance to her malady'.[19] Rumour spread inaccurately that she had died with her head on her father's Bible, open at 'Come unto me, all ye that travail and are heavy laden and I will give ye peace'.[20]

Elizabeth had not much to leave but she bequeathed a pearl necklace to Henry and a diamond ornament to the Countess of Leicester in remembrance of her time with her and the care she had received. This she had already left with the Countess perhaps knowing that her time was short. She was buried at St Thomas' Church in Newport on the Isle of Wight.

Her body embalmed and comfortably disposed of in a coffin of lead; and, after lying for sixteen days, on the 24th September was brought in a borrowed coach from the castle to the town of Newport, attended thither with her late servants. At the end of the town the corpse was met and waited on by the mayor and aldermen thereof, in all their formalities, to the church, where, about the middle of the east part of the chancel, in St. Thomas chapel, her highness was interred in a small vault purposely made, with an inscription of the date of her death engraved on her coffin. [21]

Henrietta Maria would always wear mourning in respect of the husband she had loved and lost and now there was every reason to continue in her grief.

In France, news came that Lady Dalkeith's children required her presence. Their father had died in 1649 and it was time she returned to them. Little Henrietta Anne was totally bereft at the loss of her closest companion but she could not mourn those she had not known as her mother did.

Further tragedy occurred in November when Mary lost her husband, William, to smallpox. She was absolutely devastated but she was also heavily pregnant. When she was fifteen, she had had a miscarriage but a week after William's death she gave birth to their son in a room draped black with mourning cloth. It was reported that three circles of light shone over the baby's head. Elizabeth, Queen of Bohemia, had been by her side as she would be whenever Mary was ill or had taken to her bed and recalled 'My niece is the most afflicted creature that I ever saw and is changed as she is nothing but skin and bone'.[22]

Mary wanted to call her son Charles after her father but her mother-in-law determined he should be named William for his own father as 'Charles was a name of bad augury'.[23] His care and supervision immediately put them at loggerheads and Mary would have to fight over the coming months for her right to be his guardian.

The princess at least had charge of his attendants for now. She had become much closer to Catherine Stanhope who meant much more to her than just a governess. Now she put her in charge of running William's household. Charles wrote to Stanhope from Scotland:

I have been so long and am so well acquainted with you to believe you need to be entreated to take care of my sister, especially at this time when she hath so much need. Yet because there are not many things in my power by which I may make the affection and kindness I have for her appear, and this may be one, I cannot choose but tell you I shall put the service you do her on my account… How my sister does for her health, and what discretion bears her misfortune; whether my nephew be lusty and strong, whom he is like, and a hundred such questions I desire the answer of under your hand, because a less evidence will not

*satisfy the curiosity I have for those I am so much concerned in. what
care the States take for the young General, and how kind and careful
the Princess of orange is of whom, and what provision is made for my
sister's present support I hope I shall hear from your husband.*[24]

William had named Mary regent in his will and guardian of their
son. He had raised the payment of 10,000 a year stipulated in
her dowry to 15,000 sterling and settled on her palaces at 'Buren,
Breda, Hounslardyck, and Holstein with all their furniture and
fittings-up'.[25] But over the coming months Mary's life would be
in a turmoil as her mother-in-law contested the terms of the will.
Whilst Mary claimed the regency so did she. Even the solemn
occasion of the Prince of Orange's funeral caused a dispute over
precedence between the Princes of Portugal and Mary's brother,
James, Duke of York.

Mary had grown much closer to James and leant on him for
support. In amongst all this turmoil they weren't averse to causing
mischief. When the ambassadors of the Commonwealth of England,
Walter Strickland and Oliver St. John, arrived at The Hague, they
took to riding past their residence in a disdainful manner. The
ambassadors were derided by Mary's supporters but it nearly came
to blows when James met St. John whilst out walking. James railed
at the man 'Learn, parricide, to respect the brother of your king'. 'I
scorn,' replied St. John, 'to acknowledge either you or him of whom
you speak, but as a race of vagabonds'.[26] They both went for their
swords but were stopped from bloodshed by their companions.
Mary had to send James to cool off in Breda and to add to her
concern the States ruled on 13 August 1651 that guardianship of
her son would be shared between herself, his grandmother Amelia
and Frederick William, Elector of Brandenburg. Mary had to
accept the ruling but inside she was seething.

Charles II had been crowned King of Scotland at Scone Abbey on
1 January 1651 but his restoration to the throne in England was

uncertain. The Scottish army invaded England but were defeated at the Battle of Worcester on 3 September 1651. From then on Charles was on the run. As the story goes, he once evaded capture by hiding in an oak tree at Boscobel House with Major Carlis and after six weeks of traipsing the country in disguise he managed to escape back to Holland in October. Carlis had reached Mary first and reported her brother was safe and she was overjoyed when he joined her but the governing States-General were unhappy about having an English exile in their country. Mary housed him at Teylingen, out of sight, until he could join his mother in France.

Charles had arrived with George Villers, the 2nd Duke of Buckingham, the son of Charles I's assassinated favourite, who was doing his best to cause a scandal. When Mary returned to The Hague he followed her and rumours abounded that she was considering his marriage proposal. Mary had no intention of marrying again and put it plainly 'I desire to be married only to the interests of my son'.[27] Her mother swore she would 'tear her in pieces with her own hands'[28] rather than see her marry such a man. Mary sent the love-struck duke from court but still he persisted, frequently trying to gain an audience with her, which she refused. Eventually he gave up his pursuit. Mary was happier with her next visitor, her baby brother Henry, who had been released from parliament's watch in England. Charles gave permission for him to stay with her for a time although his mother dearly wanted to see him.

Henrietta Maria, as devout as she was, wished to found a convent, somewhere where she could escape from it all and take her daughter Henrietta Anne to further her religious education. Catherine de Medici had built a country cottage on Chaillot Hill overlooking the Seine and looking for a perfect site, the queen deemed this would be an excellent place to establish it. Anne of Austria provided funds to purchase the land and signed letters-patent establishing the convent as a royal foundation. Henrietta Maria was able to furnish her own apartments there with furniture gifted from the royal palaces and when all was ready, nuns from the Convent of the Filles de Marie were invited to live there with their abbess Louise de La Fayette who was once close (perhaps too close some said) to Henrietta Maria's father, Louis XIII.

Charles was still angry about his sister's Catholicism and saw it as detrimental to his regaining the English throne. His father had specified that all his children were to be brought up as Protestants. When he couldn't get through to his mother he sent Chancellor Edward Hyde to remonstrate with her. Henrietta Maria retaliated by saying that in fact as per her marriage treaty she was given full custody of her children until they were thirteen years of age. This was true but it still did not mean that her daughter should be brought up as Catholic. The queen was adamant that Princess Henrietta Anne was a child of the French court and as such her future lay in a Catholic country.

Charles toyed with the idea of taking over his sister's care but he was still in exile with no home, no court and no stability for the little girl. Hyde at least got the queen to promise that she would not place her in a nunnery. Explaining their conversation to Charles he told him that he had suggested there was no harm in Henrietta Anne's religious upbringing staying as it was for the next three or four years as she was too young to understand it all and by which time Charles would hopefully be in a better position to look after his sister. Charles wasn't happy and Hyde wrote to the king's secretary to explain more:

I could not give better counsel or I would. Not that I was satisfied with the resolution, or will not do all in my power to alter it, by any way under heaven; yet, if by that time, the King have any place to put her in, it will easily be done; if not, I know not what to say to it. Since I could never be suspected of kindness to that religion… I think I did more than any other body… but I confess, when I spoke to the Queen and saw her passion and resolution in it, I could not advise the King what he could do, to remedy it… Tell me, I pray you, what could the King have possibly done in that business if the Queen had been willing to have delivered her to him?[29]

There was nothing Charles could do. He was in no position to take on the responsibility of his little sister and even if he had have been, the Queen was not going to give her up without a fight. Henrietta Anne would be raised in France and as a Catholic.

The French family she was part of was still enduring times of civil unrest. The second war of the Fronde was the Fronde of the Princes. Key members of the royal family; Gaston d'Orleans, Beaufort, Conti and Condé led the rebels who opposed chief minister Cardinal Mazarin and the government. Hostilities were aimed at those currently in control but the people still loved their little king. A rumour started that Louis Dieudonné, the gift of God, only twelve at the time, had been stolen from Paris and the people flocked to the Louvre demanding to see him. Anne of Austria persuaded him to feign sleep whilst some of the mob were allowed to visit his bedchamber to assure them he was safe and well. As soon as they had gone Anne took the young king to the safety of Saint-Germain. This frightening episode would stay with Louis for life and add to his dislike of Paris as his capital city.

Condé had been imprisoned but continued his plotting as soon as he was released. Leading a rebel attack on Paris in 1652 he was met by General Turenne and the royal troops at the city gates. At this point, La Grande Mademoiselle, Henrietta Maria's niece, entered the fray, on the rebels' side, to train the cannons of the Bastille on the royal troops. Mazarin had taken Louis to witness the battle and declared 'By that cannon-shot she killed her husband!' referring to the demise of any future marriage arrangements between the cousins. Mazarin knew that their dislike of him was fomenting trouble and he asked Anne of Austria to banish him to stop any further hostilities and give the Princes no reason to continue their rebellion. Condé was the only one who refused to back down and left France to return to peace whilst he joined the Spanish army.

For their part Gaston d'Orleans and La Grande Mademoiselle were banished to their countryside estates.

The fourteen-year-old Louis XIV made his state entry into Paris on 21 October 1652 and the Parisians that had risen against his government now thronged the streets to welcome him back. He did not blame his people but he would not forgive the nobility who had risen against him. In his later reign he would never 'reward princes of the blood with roles in central government'[30] and he would make Versailles not Paris the centre of his power.

For the queen dowager and Princess Henrietta Anne the return to peace saw their financial situation improved with an increased pension from the Queen of France and new apartments in the Palais-Royal, the late Cardinal Richelieu's residence, more favoured by the French court than the old Louvre, although they still preferred to spend much of their time at Saint-Germain. Henrietta Maria had asked Cromwell, soon to become Lord Protector, for a pension as queen dowager of England but he used the excuse that she had never been crowned to refuse.

Whilst her mother's situation improved, Mary was unhappy, sick and beleaguered by arguments over her son's care and inheritance. The Queen of Bohemia exhorted her to get well and enjoy herself a little. It was nearing Christmas and festivities were planned. She wrote to Charles 'My dear niece recovers her health and good looks extremely by her exercises, she twice dancing with the maskers: it has done her much good'.[31] And later also reported on a disguising they had attended 'Your sister was very well dressed, like an Amazone; the Princess Tarente like a shepherdess; Mademoiselle d'Orange like a nymph. They were all very well dressed'[32] but Mary was still having difficulties in a country she refused to call home. Her son had inherited the title of Prince of Orange from his father but had not come into his office as stadtholder of Holland mainly due to his young age. There were concerns that Mary was extremely pro-English and would influence her son to the detriment of the Dutch republic.

In the spring of 1653 William was elected stadtholder by Zeeland and other Northern provinces but Holland, under the auspices of Johan de Witt, the grand pensionary, refused to recognise him. It was true Mary firmly supported her brother's cause and gave away half of her income supporting the Royalist cause but now she endeavoured to do so secretly so as not to unsettle her son's inheritance. In May 1653 as recognition of all she had done for him Charles made Mary's son a Knight of the Garter and sent the Garter King-at-Arms to conduct the ceremony on his behalf.

Although the political situation was tedious, and gaining support for her son difficult amongst the members of the States-General, Mary's son William was extremely popular with the young boys of the United Provinces who wore orange scarfs to symbolise their support. Grand pensionary De Witt, who they saw as the prince betrayer, was on the receiving end of their taunts and they took great delight in smashing his windows. With Cromwell's acceptance of the role of Protector in December 1653, the Dutch sought to treat with England but 'the young Prince of Orange was declared incapable of ever succeeding to his father's military dignities, which were decided to be inconsistent with the safety of the republic'.[33] This new relationship between the United Provinces and the Commonwealth of England greatly upset Mary and meant her brothers would no longer be welcome at The Hague. In despair, she took herself off to her country house at Teylingen, tired of politics and yearning to see her family. Charles and James were now in France with their mother and sister and they were joined in May 1653 by Henry. The baby of the family Henrietta Anne was surrounded by all of her family except Mary and was enjoying their company. It wasn't to last.

Chapter Four

At the French Court

1654–1658

The nine-year-old Henrietta Anne made her first public appearance in February 1654 at a ball organised by Cardinal Mazarin for the marriage of his niece, Anne-Marie Martinozzi to the Prince de Conti. In April she took part in the ballet *The Nuptials of Thetis and Peleus* at the Theatre du Petit Bourbon. Here Louis XIV made his appearance as Apollo, the sun-god – he would ever be known as the Sun King and as Louis came into his own his love of theatre, dance and music would become legendary. This day he was surrounded by nine muses and after his piece Henrietta Anne stepped forward, crowned with roses and myrtle, as the muse of love and poetry, to recite her lines flawlessly. It would be the start of many appearances she would make. Her love of drama and song made her the perfect attribute to Louis' theatrics as she grew to become 'a thoroughly French princess'.[1]

Her mother was not as keen to attend these performances and as her convent was completed at Chaillot she spent more and more time there taking her daughter with her. But the queen of France was worried that Henrietta Anne was missing out on her youth. Anne endeavoured to take Princess Henrietta under her wing and even considered her suitability as a bride for Louis. Though the young king didn't look twice at his Stuart relative, as young as she was, and was avidly pursuing Marie Mancini, the youngest of Mazarin's nieces. However Anne still made sure that the princess was often at court, collecting her from the quietness of the convent to spend time with the royal family.

Mary meanwhile was to spend a happy few months with

Charles throughout the summer and autumn of 1654. She took the waters at Spa in the Ardennes Mountains and visited the baths at Aix-la-Chapelle. Charles' finances were in a bad way and Mary paid for their food and lodgings. Together they visited the cathedral where Mary kissed Charles the Great's skull then they travelled on to Cologne and Dusseldorf. One of Cromwell's spies was watching their progress and wrote of them at Cologne

> R. C. [Charles], the Princess-royal, and many others, lodged in a Protestant widow's house called Cidalbourg, where the ambassadors of Holland used to lie; a very fair and curious house, full of decent rooms and with pleasant gardens. The senate sent two hundred musketers to give R. C. three volleys of shot at his door after his arrival, and did him much honour. He and his sister, Saturday last, were invited by the Jesuits to their college, where they had a comedy prepared for them and a banquet after; but the royal brother and sister only eat some grapes standing, and drank two glasses of wine.[2]

Before long Mary returned to Teylingen Castle to see her son and Charles returned to Cologne for the winter. It was here he heard some appalling news about their brother Henry.

Henry had been living in Paris with his mother who had been delighted with her youngest son, her little Cavalier, so much like his father. Not so his tutor Richard Lovell or Lord Hatton who believed Henry would 'contract so great a rudeness (besides other vices) as may be very troublesome and incorrigible another day'.[3] His mother dismissed Lovell feeling it was he who was the bad influence and sent Henry to the abbey of Saint-Martin in Pontoise, outside of Paris. Charles was in Cologne and furious when he heard what his mother had planned for Henry. His sister may be a lost cause for now where religion was concerned but he would not allow his brother to become a Catholic.

In November, he wrote an enraged and strongly worded

letter to his brother:

> ... *you tell me that Mr Montagu, the Abbot of Pontoise, has endeavoured to pervert you from your religion. I do not doubt but you remember very well, the commands I left with you at my going away concerning that point. I am confident that you will observe them; yet your letters that come from Paris say, that it is the Queen's purpose to do all she can to change your religion, in which, if you hearken to her, or to anybody else in that matter, you must never think to see England or me again; and whatsoever mischief shall fall on me or my affairs from this time, I must lay all upon you as being the cause of it. Therefore consider well what it is to be, not only the cause of ruining a brother who loves you so well, but also your king and country. Do not let them persuade you either by force or fair promises; the first they never dare nor will use, and for the second, as soon as they have perverted you, they will have their end, and then they will care no more for you.*
>
> *I am also informed there is a purpose to put you to the Jesuits' college which I command you, on the same grounds never to consent unto; and whensoever anybody goes to dispute with you in religion, do not answer them at all; for though you have reason on your side yet they, being prepared, will have the advantage of anybody that is not upon the same familiarity with argument as they are. If you do not consider what I say unto you, remember the last words of your dead father, which were, to be constant in your religion, and never to be shaken in it; which if you do not observe this shall be the last time you will hear from, ... your most affectionate brother.*[4]

Poor Henry did as he was told and refused to go to the Jesuit College. It caused a huge falling out with his mother who disgusted by his wilfulness responded by telling him she never wanted to see him again. Charles' friend, the Marquis of Ormonde, who had also been loyal to his father was sent to collect Henry and take him to his brother in Germany. Henry asked for his mother's blessing but she refused leaving him bereft on the steps of the Palais-Royal. He could not go without saying goodbye to his sister and when he knew his mother was safely in chapel, he crept back to see her. Henrietta Anne was extremely distressed by the whole situation and was reported to cry out 'Oh me, my brother! Oh me, my mother! What shall I do? I am undone for ever'.[5] She would never see him again.

Mary was informed of the situation by Chancellor Hyde and she responded 'I give you as many thanks for your letter as I wish myself ways to hinder this misfortune that is likely to fall upon our family by my brother Harry's being made a Papist. I received a letter from my brother this last week; all the counsel I was able to give him was to resolve to obey his Majesty's orders, and not to let his tutor go from him without the king's leave. This last, I fear, he has not been able to perform'.[6] Henry must have poured his woes out to her as he arrived to stay with her for a time.

Charles also needed to visit his sister. He needed money and wrote to Mary:

> I write to you now upon a business I think I never wrote to you before upon in my life, and I never was more unwilling to do it than now. It is of money, of which, I believe, you are not much better provided than myself; yet I cannot but tell you that I am like, within a few days, to have a good occasion offered me, upon which, if I can lay hold, I may lay a foundation to compass all my business, and truly, if I am not able, I may feel the inconvenience long. I know you are without money, and cannot very easily borrow it, at least upon so little warning; but, if you will send me any jewel that I may pawn for 1500l. sterling, I do promise you, you shall have the jewel again in your hands before Christmas, and I shall be able to make a journey that I think will do my business. This is only between you and me, and I do not desire it should be known to anybody else, and if you think I may pass through the States' dominions incognito,

without giving them offence, I can take some such place in my way
as I may conveniently see you. Let me know your mind as soon as
may be.[7]

Mary thought that Charles would be welcome in Teylingen on
his way to Zeeland but she received a strict telling off from the
States-General 'we cannot in anywise believe, nor, according to
the wisdom and discretion of the above-mentioned lord-king,
expect that either he should desire or dare to take upon him to
resort into the limits of this state, and to be within the province
of Holland and West Friesland, contrary to the treaty of peace
made last year with the commonwealth of England'.[8] They
seemingly had overlooked the fact that Henry was there but not
for long. She began to receive letters instructing her to dismiss
him and when rumours emerged that the States were actually
considering putting him in custody, he was sent to Charles who
was back in Cologne. In July she joined them there but was ill
for several weeks. By September she rallied and attended the
Frankfurt Fair with Charles and Henry, a yearly event that drew
crowds of around 40,000 people to view goods from around the
world. It was supposed to be a secret but as Charles wrote to
their aunt Elizabeth 'it is so great a secret that not above halfe the
towne of Collen (Cologne) knows it… I am just now beginning
this letter in my sister's chamber, where there is such a noise
that I never hope to end it… I shall only tell your Majesty that
we are now thinking how to pass our time, in which we find two
difficulties, the one for the want of the fiddlers, the other for
somebody both to teach and assist the dancing'.[9]

But returning home, Mary was still unwell although she was
planning her next visit to her brother. The princess would spend
a lot of her time travelling between Breda and Bruges to see
Charles and it would take a toll on her health.

If I forgot to let you know of my receiving your letter, written the

Tuesday after you were returned to Cologne, you must not wonder at it; for in earnest I have not been well since I came home, and I know nothing so well able to cure me as to see you in Flanders, which I am very sorry to find is not so near as you expected when we parted; 'tis so late now that I humbly beg your pardon if I do not say much at this time; for truly, writing troubles my head, and I must give a little relation to the doctor of my health; for now from the green sickness I begin to fancy I shall fall into a consumption, though none is of my opinion; which I believe they disguise, because they would put that fancy out of my head that can do me no good.[10]

Her aunt thought the best remedy for Mary was to get outside and chop wooden billets! It's doubtful she took her advice and Mary had more worries when she upset her mother by wanting to employ Anne Hyde, the daughter of Chancellor Hyde, as her maid of honour. Henrietta Maria detested Hyde. They had a long history of animosity and to give his daughter any honours was beyond what the queen dowager considered acceptable. The chancellor too didn't really wish his daughter to take a position in Mary's household but she persisted. Her mother wrote several letters asking her to dismiss the girl but Mary enjoyed her company and refused to get rid of her. She had few pleasures and Anne helped to brighten her days. Finally her mother relented and instead asked Mary to visit her in France.

There were many who thought that Mary should not embark on an extended trip outside of the provinces, Charles included, who wrote several letters to convince her otherwise. She replied to him, 'Before I write to satisfy you with my going into France, give me leave to tell you, that not without trouble, I must complain of your usage of me, in this particular, which I had no reason to expect from so good a brother; for I do not find, by your letters, that since I came from Cullen [Cologne] you have had any new occasion to think my going to see the Queen prejudicial to your affair with the Spaniards'.[11] The princess was sick of Holland and relished the thought of attending the Sun King's court. Rumours that she meant to marry the French king were unfounded and just added to her need to escape for a while.

Her younger sister Henrietta Anne for one was growing up there although her mother closely monitored her upbringing and ensured she spent much time in her devotions. In strict contrast Queen Anne continued to bring her to balls and court gatherings. One such occurred in the winter of 1655. Anne still considered the Stuart princess a match for her son and urged Louis to take her hand for the first dance as etiquette dictated. Instead Louis took the hand of another of the cardinal's nieces, the Duchesse de Mercoeur, the eldest Mancini sister, and told his mother that he did not like little girls. Henrietta Maria tried to soothe the situation by saying her daughter was unable to dance anyway as she had hurt her foot but Anne declared that in that case the king should not dance either. Sulkily he obeyed his mother and led Henrietta Anne to the floor after all. Louis saw nothing in the princess to attract him – for now.

Mary arrived in February 1656 and finally met her sister Henrietta Anne for the first time. The French court welcomed her, allocating her sumptuous apartments in the Palais-Royal and made every effort to ensure she was well entertained. Two days after her arrival, Louis XIV's brother Philippe, the duke of Anjou, held a ball in the Salle des Gardes in Mary's honour. The king led Henrietta Anne out to open the ball sparking further rumours they might eventually marry but it was Mary that the French nobles were entranced with. She 'outdid all our court, though it had never been fuller of fine women'.[12] Mary was in her element. She had ever disliked Holland and France was marvellous in her eyes. Her social calendar was full with rounds of masques, ballets, dinners and balls which quite wore their mother out but thrilled the Stuart sisters. Mary, as a widow, was not allowed to take part in the dancing although she longed to but Henrietta Anne made sure she made up for it. Mary wrote to Charles:

> I have seen the masque again, and in the entry of the performances received another present, which was a petticoat of cloth of silver, embroidered with Spanish leather, which is very fine and very extraordinary; for the first present, I make no doubt but you have heard of it; therefore I say nothing of it. I was, since that, at a supper at the chancellor's, where the king and queen and all the court were, which was really extremely fine. Two nights ago the king came here in masquerade, and others, and danced here. Monday next there is a little ball at the Louvre, where I must dance; judge, therefore, in what pains I shall be. This is all I have to say, for I have been this day at the Carmelites, and, to confess the truth, am a little weary.[13]

The visit to the Convent had been another move by Queen Henrietta Maria to convert one of her children to Catholicism but Mary would have none of it. She did agree to attend one Catholic ceremony to see an English lady take the veil at Chaillot but that was as far as she would go with regard to her mother's wishes who was worn out with the attention her daughter was receiving. She told Charles that Mary had been so overwhelmed with visitors 'that I am dead with it'.[14]

Mary and her mother along with a large escort of nobles took time out to visit La Grande Mademoiselle, still banished to the countryside after her involvement in the Fronde, who thought the Dowager Princess of Orange was quite the thing. She may have been in mourning and wearing customary black but was adorned with 'the most beautiful diamond earrings I ever beheld, very fine pearls, clasps and large diamond bracelets, with splendid rings of the same'.[15] It took a lot to impress Henrietta Maria's niece and she was known more for her scathing tongue than for compliments but Mary stood out. La Grande Mademoiselle wrote in her memoirs that she had asked Mary how she liked the French court. She replied 'She was indeed well pleased with it – the more so because she had a great aversion to that of Holland; and that as soon as her brother Charles was settled in any place, she should go and live with him'.[16]

Mary stayed throughout the summer until she heard her young son had caught smallpox. Although he appeared to be recovering, she decided it was time to return home and after tears and hugs of farewell from her family and her new friends at the French court she began her journey to The Hague stopping to see Charles in Bruges on her way back. Mary always loved seeing her brother and this time was no exception but as soon as she was home she began receiving angry letters from him.

Charles had signed a treaty with the Spanish in April but felt that Mary's friends, Lord and Lady Balcarres were undermining his policies by treating with the French with Mary's support. The princess strongly denied his accusation saying it was 'as false as those who report it of me'.[17] Mary had done so much for her brother, providing him with money and giving his supporters a place to stay. She had taken Jane Lane, the woman who had helped him escape from England, into her household but Charles was still unhappy with her.

Charles wrote to her again concerning rumours that she was having an affair with Henry Jermyn, equerry to her brother James. Rumours even abounded that they had secretly married. Charles ordered his immediate dismissal and Mary annoyed at his interference and for believing the rumours in the first place wrote:

Now that you see how exactly you are obeyed, I hope you will give me leave to desire you to consider, what consequences your severity will bring upon me. To justify any of my actions to you, on this occasion, were, I think, to do as much wrong to both my brothers as to my own innocency, since they have been witnesses of what some person's insolency, has dared to represent unto you as faults. Therefore, I leave it to them and only think of what will now reflect upon me, which as I have the honour to be your sister, you ought to consider, and not to make a public discourse of what can neither prove for your honour nor mine. I am so willing to think you only try to what a degree my obedience is to you, that I cannot persuade myself you will not, now, give my brother, the Duke of York, leave to send for Mr. Jermyn back, which will not only stop malicious tongues, but give me the happiness of seeing that you take a kindly, as well as a brotherly interest in me.[18]

While Mary was seething in Holland, her sister Henrietta Anne was now growing into a young lady lauded by those at the French court. Mary's visit had propelled her into the limelight and those that had not noticed her before did so now. Father Cyprien wrote of her as 'a princess of extraordinary merit, not only for the graces and beauties of mind, with which nature, prodigal of its gifts, has most liberally enriched her, but much more for the holiness of religion, and the sentiments of piety that heaven has shed abroad in her heart'.[19] He was not the only one to praise her. Madame de la Serre, royal historiographer of France, also praised her virtues.

Her figure is rich, her bearing grave, her hair most beautiful, her brow a mirror, representing the majesty of her race, and her eyes matchless; in short, the sun sees nothing to equal her. The beauty of her soul can only be compared to that of her countenance. Her disposition is so good that from the moment of first learning to follow virtue, she needed no other guide. She speaks so agreeably that the pleasure of hearing her is no less than that of seeing her: in singing, echo alone can equal her, and in other accomplishments she is unrivalled. She has the mind, the voice, the beauty of an angel; let it not be thought strange if Heaven enriches her with its rare treasures. Who can express her goodness, grace, sweetness, and wisdom? She possesses a thousand other qualities; least of all is that of princess.[20]

Although she shone when she was at court she still spent most of her time with her mother, Henrietta Maria, between their apartments at the Palais-Royal, the convent at Chaillot and in 1657, at their country house in Colombes, north of Paris which the queen dowager had purchased from the Fouquet family with money from Queen Anne. They also took the waters at Bourbon-aux-Bains for a month each summer for their health. When they were at court some still saw them as the poor relatives as demonstrated by La Grande Mademoiselle when she was back in favour. In 1658, at a fete held by Chancellor Seguier, Mademoiselle, ignoring etiquette, went into dinner before the princess, earning her the displeasure of Queen Anne who was always mindful of the Stuarts. But some felt she was in the right – Philippe, Duke of Anjou, who always sided with La Grande Mademoiselle snidely commented 'Things must come to a fine pass, if we are to allow people who depend upon us for bread to pass before us. For my part, I think they had better betake themselves elsewhere'.[21] But Philippe was soon to change his mind regarding Henrietta Anne.

Mary had managed to meet up with Charles at Antwerp and invited James and Henry to the fair at The Hague in the summer but again the States-General informed her they were not welcome. Their relationship with England's Commonwealth was too precious for them to jeopardise but when Cromwell died on 3 September 1658 James and Henry visited her once more in disguise to ask for her advice. All eyes were on England and what would happen. Charles too was considering the possibilities and one was to make an alliance with Holland through his marriage to the daughter of Mary's mother-in-law, Henrietta Catharine.

The winter of 1658 saw Mary enraged with Charles for even contemplating such a move. Rarely did the siblings fall out even though the past years had been a trial but this was too much for her to bear.

Oliver Cromwell

Chapter Five

Marriage to the Duke

1659–1661

Henrietta Anne was fifteen in the summer of 1659. Her mother wanted an advantageous marriage for her but suitors were uncertain of this Stuart princess, half French, half English with a brother still anxiously trying to gain his throne. She was of royal blood but she was impoverished. Marrying a poor princess also meant marrying into her family and many were aware that Charles II needed funds for his cause. She was currently an unknown quantity but she certainly had many attributes as Madame de Brégis wrote gushingly:

> *I must tell you that this young Princess is still growing and that she will soon attain a perfect staure. Her air is as noble as her birth, her hair is of a brightest chestnut hue, and her complexion rivals that of the gayest flowers. The snowy whiteness of her skin betrays the lilies from which she sprang. Her eyes are blue and brilliant, her lips ruddy, her throat beautiful, her arms and hands well made. Her charms show that she was born on a throne, and is destined to return there. Her wit is lively and agreeable. She is admired in her serious moments and beloved in her most ordinary ones; she is gentle and obliging, and her kindness of heart will not allow her to laugh at others, as cleverly as she could if she chose. She spends most of her time in learning, all that can make a princess perfect, and devotes her spare moments to the most varied accomplishments. She dances with incomparable grace, she sings like an angel, and the spinet is never so well played as by her fair hands...*[1]

And Sir John Reresby, a Royalist, who visited the French court also spoke highly of her.

As I spoke the language of the country, and danced pretty well, the young princess, then about fifteen years of age, behaved towards me with all the civil freedom that might be; she made me dance with her, played on the harpsichord to me in her highness's chamber, suffered me to wait on her as she walked in the garden, and sometimes to toss her in a swing between two trees, and, in fine, to be present at all her innocent diversions.[2]

For all these compliments, she still needed to marry. Henrietta Maria hoped that with their family ties that Louis XIV would still take her for a bride and although Queen Anne thought much of her and had considered the possibility, she really wished her son to marry her Spanish niece, Marie-Therese to put an end to years of French hostilities with Spain. Although personally Louis was still happy to chase Marie Mancini, his mother saw that with the signing of the Treaty of the Pyrenees, his marriage to her niece might now be arranged.

In November, Henrietta Anne wrote to her brother – the first surviving letter we have of an ongoing correspondence and mutual affection between the siblings as she grew up. Henrietta wrote in French, Charles in English. In it she hoped that 'peace will give you all the happiness you desire'[3] referring to the Treaty and sent wishes to see him soon. Charles had been in Fuenterrabia at the peace negotiations but he returned to France in December and met with his family at Colombes. It was a quiet Christmas with many of the court having accompanied Louis XIV to Spain to meet his bride. It had been five years since Henrietta Anne had seen her brother and she had changed so much that Charles didn't recognise her. Instead he went to greet another girl who was there until his mistake was pointed out. Just a little embarrassed, he embraced his sister amazed at her transformation. This visit cemented their relationship and although they would live in separate countries they would ever be close.

In February 1660 Charles wrote to her from Brussels where Mary, having forgiven him for even thinking of marrying Amelia's daughter, had joined him. He told Henrietta Anne '... I will never give up the friendship I have for you, and you give me so many marks of yours that we shall never have another quarrel but as to which of us shall love the other most. But in this I will never yield to you'.[4] At the end of the letter he remonstrates 'please do not treat me with so much ceremony, or address me with so many Your Majesties. For between you and me there should be nothing but affection'.[5] Interestingly, for all Charles protestations about the Catholic religion he also mentions a scapular that his sister is to send him that he promises to always wear.

Charles' fortunes were looking up. Cromwell's son Richard had succeeded as Lord Protector of England, Scotland and Ireland but he resigned after only a short term. By 1660 Parliament was formally inviting Charles II to return to his throne and terms were being negotiated. For Charles' part he signed the declaration of Breda that included a general pardon for those who had committed crimes during the English Civil War and the Interregnum. There were a lot of anxious nobles who had fought against the Royalists or taken part in Charles I's downfall that wanted to know they would be safe in the new king's reign. And they would be – for the time being. Charles however would never forgive those who had signed his father's death warrant.

As Charles prepared to return to England, Mary despaired she could not go with him. She had had enough problems of her own. Mary had been regent of Orange, in her son's stead, since 1657 and had asked King Louis XIV to aid her in obtaining control of the area to 'legitimate authority, and the tranquillity, that the violence of his lordship, Count Dohna have impaired'.[6] Count Dohna, its governor, refused to cede power to her until he was offered 200,000 livres. But in Louis' enthusiasm for conquest he had not only helped but usurped her and Orange fell to French troops in March 1660.

Although she was devastated and worried about her son's inheritance, it was time to be by Charles' side as he was finally lauded as the king of England. At Breda there was a public thanksgiving for the restoration of peace in England and the next day Charles, Mary and her son, James and Henry proceeded to The Hague – this time all being welcome. James organised the procession of boats to take them by water. Charles enjoyed his trip on a yacht so much he asked for one to be made for him that would be later presented to the king and named *Mary*. His sister however was struggling with seasickness as they made their way to The Hague.

Now De Witt, who had caused Mary many problems, gave Charles an apology 'We must even admit that for some years past interest of state has done violence to our natural inclinations, since it was not in your august person that we found the representative of that country, and thus your Majesty may judge with what affection and zeal we shall in future cherish and maintain close union and close correspondence between your kingdom and this republic; since, now that we see your majesty restored, our natural inclination and the interests of the state are united'. Charles told him 'I take into consideration that you were forced to treat with people who. Having revolted against my father, were equally persistent against me; but now you will have to do with men of honour'.[7]

For several days Charles was visited by well-wishers and received money and gifts including the crown jewels that his mother had pawned in Holland. At a banquet given by states of Holland, Charles sat between his aunt Elizabeth of Bohemia and his sister Mary. Charles gave a rapturous speech and exhorted the States-General to be good to his sister and her son who was now fifth in succession to the crown of England and studying at

Leiden under Professor Bernicus. To make sure it was taken note of he also wrote:

> *My Lords, as I am leaving with you the princess my sister, and the Prince of Orange my nephew, two persons whom I esteem beyond measure, I entreat you, my lords, that you will take their interests to heart, and let them enjoy your hearty favour on all occasions in which the princess my sister may solicit it, either for herself or for the prince her son; in full assurance that all your respect and favour towards her will be recognised by me just as though I had received it in my own person.*[8]

Before long it was time for tearful goodbyes and Mary was bereft at her brother's leaving but gladdened that after years of exile he would now sit on the throne of England as their father had done. Her one consolation was that Charles promised she should join him soon and she had her son to consider. Charles' restoration meant William's prospects were restored too. Not only was in restored to the succession to the English throne but the States of Holland paid him his due and took charge of his education, restored his legal right to become stadtholder (until this would not occur until 1672) and 'withdrew his appointment as Captain and Admiral-General of the forces of the United Provinces'.[9]

After Charles left, Mary decided it was time to show her son to his people. They were warmly welcomed in Amsterdam. He toured the city on horseback and went to see the yacht the States were building for his uncle. Touchingly on his return to The Hague, a group of young boys saluted him and he welcomed them into the palace where Mary ordered refreshments and William gave them all a gingerbread cake. While William returned to his studies at Leiden, Mary began to plan her trip to England.

When Charles arrived at Canterbury, he dashed off a quick

letter to his younger sister Henrietta Anne telling her 'I arrived yesterday at Dover where I found Monk with a great number of the nobility who almost overwhelmed me with friendship and joy at my return. My head is so prodigiously dazed by the acclamation of the people and by quantities of business that I know not whether I am writing sense or no, therefore you will pardon me if I do not tell you any more, only that I am entirely yours'.[10]

On 29 May, Charles' thirtieth birthday, he rode into London with his brothers James and Henry by his side. At Whitehall, Charles greeted his people and the city celebrated his arrival. The Venetian ambassador reported 'For three days and three nights they have lighted bonfires and made merry, burning effigies of Cromwell and other rebels with much abuse. The foreign ministers have taken part in these rejoicings, and I also, in addition to the illuminations have kept before the door a fountain of wine and other liquors, according to the custom of the country, much to the delight of the people and amid acclamations'.[11]

France also celebrated the restoration of the English monarchy. Henrietta Maria wrote to her son 'I think I shall have all Paris to congratulate me. Indeed, you would never imagine what joy there is here'.[12] Nobles and royalists flocked to congratulate the queen dowager. Even those that had never lent their support now came to see her and her daughter.

Where once there had been no suitors for Henrietta Anne, now she became more attractive as the sister of the restored king of England. Louis XIV's brother, Philippe, now Duke of Orleans after the death of his uncle Gaston in February, was one of them. The duke who had made snide remarks about the poverty of his cousin these days saw her in a new light. Gifts from Charles proved that his finances were reinstated and he now had sufficient funds to look after his family in France. With his fortunes restored, he sent Henrietta Anne a magnificent side saddle of gold lace and green velvet which she adored. Suddenly his sister was a marriage prospect for some of the highest nobles in France but first there was the marriage of the French king. After months of negotiation and the French court's progress to Spain, Louis XIV married Marie-Therese, daughter of King Philip IV, by proxy on 3 June 1660 at Fuenterrabia. On the 7th Marie-Therese crossed over to the Isle of Pheasants on the Bidasoa river, the natural border between France and Spain, and then on 9 June they married in person in an ancient chapel in France at Saint-Jean-de-Luz near Bordeaux. It was a marriage of diplomacy not love. The queen mother was delighted but the other ladies secretly laughed at Marie-Therese's strange dress and quaint hairstyle. A foreign queen was always something new to behold and gossip about.

Whilst Louis and his new bride began their progress back to Paris, Philippe – known as Monsieur – was falling in love with Henrietta Anne. Philippe was the younger brother who had been kept in the shade of the Sun King. Madame de La Fayette described him as 'much disposed to the pursuits of women as the King was adverse to them. He was well made and handsome, but with a stature and type of beauty more fitting to a princess than to a prince and he had taken more pains to have his beauty admired by all the world than to enjoy it for the conquest of women despite the fact that he was continuously amongst them. His vanity, it seemed, made him incapable of affection save of himself'.[13] He liked to dress as a woman, something his mother was blamed for since she dressed him in girl's clothes from an early age, and in the bedroom he preferred same-sex relations. Something that was punishable by death but rife and overlooked at the decadent French court.

Still at this time he did appear to be totally infatuated with Henrietta Anne and held a ball in her honour at Saint-Cloud, a beautiful residence close to the Seine that his brother had not long bought for him for 240,000 livres. He led the Stuart princess out to open the ball and the night was a whirlwind of dance with those watching the couple convinced they would soon wed. Her mother thought so too and wrote to Mary at The Hague that Henrietta Anne's betrothal would soon be settled.

On 24 August the queen mother formally asked Henrietta Maria for her daughter's hand in marriage on behalf of her son Philippe. The dowager queen immediately wrote to Charles for his approval.

I arrived in this town yesterday: as soon as I got in, the queen called to see me, and informed me that she came on the part of the king, her son, to tell me that they both unitedly begged me to be pleased to approve a request they had to make of me, which was, that I would do Monsieur the honour to give him my daughter in marriage, and that they had resolved to send an ambassador to you to this effect; she also said many friendly things to me about you and myself. I answered her that the king and she would do my daughter too much honour, and that I would not fail to let you know of this proposal. I beg you to favour it. In the interim, before we can send the ambassador, I think you should give me permission to say that you approve it. I assure you that your sister is not at all displeased about it; and as to Monsieur, he is violently in love, and quite impatient for your reply.[14]

Perhaps Henrietta Anne was not displeased. It was an advantageous match but Philippe was an unusual man and his passions would prove to make their marriage a difficult one. Still that was in the future and Charles agreed to their joining even though he received other proposals for his sister from the Duke of Savoy, the King of Portugal and even Prince Rupert of the Rhine, her cousin.

With thoughts of her own marriage Henrietta Anne watched Marie-Therese's state entry into a scorching hot Paris on 26 August alongside her mother and Queen Anne from the balcony of the Hotel de Beauvais. Louis' new bride rode into the city in a golden chariot accompanied by the king riding at its right side with Philippe on the left. The procession stopped at the hotel to salute the queen mother and her honoured guests. Henrietta Anne watched on as her dashing husband-to-be passed by on his white charger.

Before any wedding ceremony Henrietta Anne's mother wished to visit England with her daughter. Whilst plans were being made they heard two pieces of news that shocked and appalled them. The first was James's marriage to Anne, the daughter of Charles' chancellor, Sir Edward Hyde and Mary's maid of honour who had seemingly met James when Mary took her to France with her. The second was the death of young Henry from smallpox whilst residing in Whitehall, both occurring in September. It made the need to go to England more urgent and they were on their way by the end of October with Father Cyprien accompanying them. They stopped at Beauvais, Crévecoeur, Poix, Abbeville and eventually Calais where they had to remain for two days until the weather was suitable for sailing.

Mary had sent for William and said her goodbyes as she prepared to head for England. On board the vice-admirals ship the *Tredagh*, which was escorted by five man-of-wars and two frigates, she was told the news of her brother Henry's death only once they had set sail, and she remained in her cabin for the crossing mourning the younger brother she had lost. She arrived before her mother and sister on 26 October and was settling in to her apartments at Whitehall. Father Cyprien recalled the queen dowager's and Henrietta Anne's journey:

They took shipping at Calais in English vessels, in which the highest nobles of the court of England had come to compliment and accompany the Queen on behalf of the King, her son. I know not if there was ever seen so dead a calm, which made the sea look like glass; the wind was so completely at rest, that the sails of the ships, deprived of the desirable breezes, kept those large vessels motionless. In spite of all the efforts of the crews, it took two days to cross from Calais to Dover, though the distance is so short that, with a fair wind, it may be per formed in three hours. The Duke of York, high-admiral, came to receive the queen, his mother, with the whole fleet, composed of such a multitude of ships, and ranged in such a manner, that their masts appeared like large trees, and resembled a spacious wood. When on board, the guns began to thunder; each ship firing in its turn and order, one after another, they kept up a noise marvellously loud and delightful, which lasted for a good half hour, at Calais and at Dover. All the rarest and the most exquisite viands rendered the supper sumptuous, not only for the Queen and for Madame her daughter, but likewise for all those who enjoyed it, gratifying the palate and satisfying that craving hunger which the calm sea air had produced. This regale was at the cost of the Duke of York, who knew that we were fasting. It was then Lent: in order to obtain an exemption for it, he had the goodness to come to us, and said, 'I have heard that, at this time, you do not eat meat, and that you are fasting; you will fare ill, for not only have we no supply of fish, but all these people are Huguenots, who will not do what they might to treat you well; but, while I am speaking, I recollect that we have some sturgeon here. I will go and order it to be given to you. We returned warm thanks to that prince, in admiration of his rare kindness. On approaching Dover, the King came to meet the Queen, his mother: the respect, the attentions, and all the testimonies of perfect joy which he paid her, may be better imagined than described. In this excess of joy, and in delightful conversations, the ships advanced and arrived at Dover, where the King had prepared festivities of extra ordinary magnificence for his honoured mother, for the princess, his sister, and for all their retinues, whose expenses he defrayed.[15]

Now in Dover, Henrietta Anne greeted her brother Charles with warmth and affection. James was there and Mary too. After a sumptuous banquet in the evening they rose early the next day to begin their journey to London passing through Canterbury and Rochester. It was all new to Henrietta. She had left England when she was two, was now sixteen, and only had very vague recollections of her country of birth supported by the stories her mother told her. The people were delighted to have her back on English soil and waved and cheered her progress to London. The queen dowager had refused a formal entry by water into the city. Instead they rode to Whitehall arriving on the 12 November.

Too tired the next day, Henrietta Anne stayed in her rooms dressed in a night gown covered with an Indian robe with a mob cap perched on her head. James and Mary joined her for a game of ombre. She received the Comte de Soissons, the French ambassador, who would later approach Charles to finalise the negotiations for her marriage to Philippe. An Italian envoy, Marquis Pallavicino, arrived around the same time to ask for her hand for the Duke of Savoy but was politely turned down.

Her marriage to Philippe was now advancing. It was negotiated that Henrietta Anne was to receive a dowry of £40,000 from Charles with a further gift of £20,000 towards her marriage expenses. Louis agreed to support her with a yearly income of 40,000 livres and the Chateau de Montargis as a gift. Mary too had been allowed a £40,000 dowry but it had never been paid. Henrietta may have been more trusting but Mary knew how money promised had a way of never arriving.

Parliament offered both Mary and Henrietta Anne a payment of £10,000. Mary received hers but Henrietta Anne never saw a penny. She would later tell Ralph Montagu, the English ambassador in France that 'the king made bold with it and she never had a farthing of it'.[16] But she was happy for Charles to use it. She had plenty and would have more when she married the duke. Her mother was also allowed a £30,000 yearly income from Parliament which Charles said he would match. Their days of poverty were over.

Her stay in England was an exciting one with new people to meet, balls and entertainments. Henrietta Anne received special attention from George Villiers, 2nd Duke of Buckingham who had once been besotted with her sister and was now absolutely enamoured with her. When Philippe heard the news in France he was furious. He was anxiously awaiting the return of his bride-to-be, fretting that she may never come back to him.

Not everyone was as complimentary as others had been. Pepys, the famous diarist, caustically described the queen mother and her daughter – 'the queen a very little, plain old woman, and nothing more in her presence in any respect nor garb than an ordinary woman... The Princess Henrietta is very pretty but much below my expectation, and her dressing of herself with her hair frizzed short up to her ears, did make her seem so much the less to me. But my wife standing near her with two or three black patches on, and well dressed, did seem to me much handsomer than she'.[17]

None of this mattered when Mary became ill. She had been complaining of pains in her chest due to the smokiness of the city but her illness worsened. Lord Craven wrote to inform the Queen of Bohemia:

I believe your majesty will hear the hot alarum of the princess royal's being in great danger of death, which, indeed, this morning was sadly apprehended by many; but because your majesty should not be frighted at what news perchance you may hear, I have just now been with her, and, God be praised, she is much better. The doctors do not yet know whether it is the pox or the measles, but I fear it will prove the small-pox.[18]

It was indeed smallpox. Henrietta Anne was immediately moved to St James' Palace to keep her safe and barred from seeing her sister. Twenty-nine-year-old Mary seemed to be rallying but after being weakened by blood-letting she collapsed and died on Christmas Eve 'to the intense grief of the whole court and especially the king, who loved her most tenderly'.[19] Knowing she was dying she had written a will. Her main concern was her son:

I earnestly beseech his majesty, as also the queen, my royal mother, to take upon them the care of the Prince of Orange, my son, as the best parents and friends I can commend him unto, and from whom he is, with most reason, to expect all good helps, both at home and abroad, praying to God to bless and make him a happy instrument to his glory, and to his country's good, as well as to the satisfaction and advantage of his nearest friends and allies.[20]

Lord Chesterfield who was with her when she died wrote of her, 'I could not but admire her unconcernedness, constancy of mind and resolution, which well began the grandchild of Henry the Fourth of France'.[21] Charles would later sign a treaty with Holland regarding William's guardianship. Although Mary would never see it her son would live to become King William III of England. The States-General immediately wrote to Charles with their condolences and while they mourned her loss, Mary was carried in state from Somerset House to Westminster Abbey.

First went gentlemen and knights, next the servants of the Duke of York, then the servants of the Queen, after whom came his majesty's servants, next those of the deceased lady. Then two heralds before the Duke of Ormonde, lord-steward of his majesty's household, then Edward Earl of Manchester, lord chamberlain, after whom came Edward Earl of Clarendon, Lord Chancellor of England, with the purse and macebearer before him. Then came another herald bearing the coronet of her royal high ness, Princess-royal of England and Princess-dowager of Orange, on a cushion of black velvet, followed by the remains of the royal lady, carried by her own servants; the pall being supported by six earls, and the canopy over it carried by baronets. His royal highness, the Duke of York, preceded by another herald, followed the corpse of his royal sister as chief mourner; his train was supported by persons of very high rank. In this order they came to Henry VII.'s chapel, where the remains of Mary Princess-royal of England, Princess-dowager of Orange, were interred in the vault of the royal Stuart line, beside those of Henry Duke of Gloucester.[22]

William of course had to be told and Elizabeth, Queen of Bohemia went to comfort him in his grieving as she suffered in hers. Even Charles Louis, who had once claimed Mary should be his bride, wrote to his mother 'I am sorry for this new affliction God hath sent on your royal family; whereof I am the more sensible because I know how near it toucheth your majesty's affection, which was ever great towards the deceased Princess, of whom you will ever find the want while you stay at The Hague. I pray God to comfort your majesty in all this great afiliction, and to_do me such grace that I may be able to contribute something—if not so much as my duty requires towards it.'[23]

After Mary's burial next to her brother the queen dowager made immediate plans to take Henrietta Anne back to France. Philippe was writing letters to Henrietta Maria urging their return as he was concerned for her health. Louis had joked with him he would be marrying the 'bones of the holy innocents'[24] referring to the princess's delicate figure and piety. Philippe feared that bones she may be if she wasn't back in France soon.

The queen dowager had been appalled by James' marriage to Anne Hyde, the Chancellor's daughter, but Mary's death must have had a softening effect on her for she dined with her new daughter-in-law before they left London. Charles had refused to let his brother out of the marriage anyway and the king had his own nuptials to consider.

On 9 January 1661 the queen dowager and Henrietta Anne sailed from Portsmouth on the *London*. The duke of Buckingham managed to get permission to accompany them but was driving

Henrietta mad with his attentions. When a storm developed and Henrietta became ill, they returned to Portsmouth. It was feared that the smallpox had followed them on board but Charles sent two of his doctors to confirm it was in fact measles. They sailed again on 25 January but still it took six days to reach Le Havre.

They stayed in the town for a few days, sending the annoying Duke of Buckingham on to tell Philippe and the king of their arrival, then were escorted through Normandy by its governor, the Duc de Longueville, on to the abbey of St Martin near Pontoise where Louis and Philippe were anxiously awaiting their arrival. Philippe joined them for their journey to Paris where they received an official welcome at St Denis before retiring to the Palais-Royal. The duke noticed Buckingham's over-attentiveness and immediately wrote to Charles to make him recall the man who was annoying the princess. The ballet *L'Impatience des Amoureux* was given in Henrietta's honour. Louis had organised it as a humorous nod to Philippe's impatience to marry and he would still have to wait.

The queen dowager sighed with relief when they finally arrived at the convent of Chaillot although it must have been suddenly too quiet for Henrietta after their recent travels. As Philippe and herself were cousins they had to wait for Papal dispensation for their marriage which arrived on 9 March. On the same day Cardinal Mazarin died and their wedding had to be delayed by a period of mourning but by the end of the month their marriage contract was signed and Henrietta Anne and Philippe were betrothed in the Palais-Royal in front of the King and Queen of France and the two queen dowagers, Henrietta Maria and Anne, surrounded by the leading nobles of the French court.

Their marriage was solemnised the next day in the chapel with Monsieur de Cosnac, the Bishop of Valence and Grand Almoner to the duke, presiding. Philippe had wanted an extravagant wedding in Notre Dame but due to Mazarin's death it was a much smaller affair but still celebrated in style.

Louis wrote to Charles the following day:

> *Since I have always considered the marriage of my brother with your sister, the Princess of England, as a new tie which would draw still closer the bonds of our friendship, I feel more joy than I can express, that it was yesterday happily accomplished; and as I doubt not that this news will inspire you with the same sentiments as I feel myself, I would not delay one moment to share my joy with you, nor would I lose the opportunity of this mutual congratulation, to tell you that I am, my brother, very truly your good brother.*[25]

Henrietta Anne would now be known as Madame at the French court as her husband was Monsieur. L'abbé de Choisy wrote of this time:

> *Never has France had a Princess as attractive as Henriette d'Angleterre, when she became the wife of Monsieur. Never was there a Princess so fascinating, and so ready to please all who approached her. Her eyes were black and brilliant, full of the fire which kindles a prompt response in other hearts... She had all the wit to make a woman charming, and what is more, all the talent necessary for conducting important affairs, had this been required of her. But at the court of our young King in those days, pleasure was the order of the day, and to be charming was enough.*[26]

This may have been true for now but both Charles and Louis were well aware that Henrietta's marriage had forged a solid link between England and France, one that would be tried and tested over the coming years.

For Henrietta Anne her honeymoon period was the first time since her arrival in France that she had been separated from her mother – and she didn't want to go with her husband to the Tuileries, the sumptuous addition to the Louvre added by Catherine de Medici, though she knew she had to. Father Cyprien wrote:

When Monsieur came to fetch this princess to take her to his apartments in the Tuileries, there was general mourning in the Palais Royal; sighs, tears and sobs of the Queen and Madame, made some weep, melted the hearts of others and pained all.[27]

Still she was the centre of attention with frequent visits from the court nobles and the king himself. Ladies now flocked to her, anxious to be with the new duchess, and receive her favours. Henrietta Anne surrounded herself with female companions – the duchess of Chatillon (an old flame of her brothers), Mademoiselle de Mortemart, Madame de Monaco and the Marquise de La Fayette who would later write her memoirs. It was as well she had their support as Philippe soon grew bored with her. The chase had been his fun. Now she was his wife he became disinterested, later admitting that just two weeks after their marriage he was no longer in love with her.

Henrietta was able to visit her mother in May at Colombes before visiting Saint-Cloud with her husband. It was one of her favourite residences where she enjoyed the gardens with her ladies, took daily coach rides, went horse riding and swam in the river.

Philippe always conscious of the hold his brother had over him became jealous of the attention the king was paying his wife. The queen had been ill and so it was Henrietta as the second lady of France who stepped in to take her place at the ceremony of the washing of the feet on Holy Thursday and on other occasions throughout that summer. When the court moved to Fontainebleau Louis wrote to her:

If I wish myself at St Cloud it is not because of its grottos or the freshness of its foliage. Here we have gardens fair enough to console us, but the company which is there now, is so good, that I find myself furiously tempted to go there, if I did not expect to see you tomorrow, I do not know what I should do and could not help making a journey to see you. Remember me to all your ladies, and do not forget the affection that I have promised you, which is, I can assure you, all you could possibly desire, if indeed you wish me to love you very much.[28]

Their closeness was becoming quite the talk of the court. After Mazarin's death, the twenty-two-year-old Louis had more control than ever and this summer was one of celebration and decadence. With the queen still ill and Louis having no interest in her anyway, the king spent more and more time with Henrietta. He led her out as the principal woman at court to open balls, cast her in roles opposite himself for the entertainments and joined her on a barge in the evenings so they could take in the cool air of the canal. In June the Duke of Beaufort held a ball and nine days of entertainment followed after with the king and Henrietta as hosts.

It was rumoured they were lovers but no one knew for sure.

Philippe may have been bored with his wife but neither did he want his brother to have her. He complained to his mother who had also noticed the growing feelings between her eldest son and her daughter-in-law. Queen Anne spoke to Queen Henrietta Maria about her daughter's behaviour. Once they had conspired to bring the couple together. Now they were married to their respective partners it would not do.

The royal couple knew they would have to devise something to put people off and concocted a plan for Louis to be known to have taken a new mistress. They thought that Louise de La Valliere, one of Henrietta's maids of honour, would do and if they were seen often together no one would suspect Louis' relationship with his brother's wife. Although Louis paid homage to Henrietta in the end of season ballet, her plan had misfired. Louise had indeed become his mistress.

It may have pained Henrietta but she was not without her own admirers. The brother of her close friend, Madame de Monaco, became more than a little enamoured with her. The Comte de Guiche, eldest son of the Maréchal de Gramont, also a favourite of her husband's pressed his suit, and she encouraged his flirtation until that too became the talk of the court and Philippe ordered him to desist. Henrietta Anne was feeling ill and didn't have the energy anyway. It soon became apparent she was pregnant but she had been invited as guest of honour to Nicholas Fouquet's ball on the 17 August fete at Vaux-le-Vicomte and she would attend albeit on a litter carried by two footmen. Fouquet, the Superintendent of Finances, put on a lavish display with a performance of Moliere's comedy *Les Facheux* and extravagant fireworks. Mazarin had warned Louis against the man. He was too extravagant – for his display of wealth led Louis to question where it had all come from and just weeks later he would be arrested and imprisoned in Pignerol fortress.

The Queen of France gave birth to a boy on 1 November at Fontainebleau. Spanish music played under her window during her twelve-hour labour. The dauphin was called Louis after his father and both mother and child were thriving. Henrietta's health however was not improving. She lost weight, had a wracking cough and was taking opium to ease her pain. Rest would improve her situation and the loving message she received from Charles in December helped to fortify her:

> *I have been in very much paine for your indisposition, not so much that I thought it dangerous, but for fear that you should miscarry. I hope now that you are out of that fear too, and for God's sake, my dearest sister have a care for yourselfe...*[29]

This was the first letter in which he refers to her as Minette or pussy cat, his pet name for her. Henrietta was slowly recovering and wrote back to Charles with the latest gossip but also an early attempt at involving herself in matters of state. Louis was unhappy that English man-of-war ships received a salute from foreign vessels. The French king was jealous of the English fleet and wanted a fleet of his own and one that would be saluted for being French. It was a petty trifle but could have turned into a worse argument. Charles could not even believe that Louis would be troubled by it.

> *This is a right so well known and never disputed by any king before… I hope what you say to me is only your fears, for I will never believe that anybody who desires my friendship will expect that which was never so much as thought of before. Therefore, all I shall say to you is, that my ships must do their duties, let what will happen of it. And I should be very unworthy if I quit a right and go lower than ever any of my predecessors did. Which is all I have to say, only that I am very glad to find you so well recovered, and be assured, my dearest sister, that I am entirely yours.*[30]

The siblings would soon be involved in far more difficult negotiations.

Chapter Six

Plays, Ballets & Intrigues

1662–1664

Henrietta Anne was told by her doctor to rest through the winter, to recover and protect the baby she was carrying. She used the time to correspond with her brother. Charles' marriage to the Portuguese Catherine of Braganza was being arranged and one of the ladies Henrietta had grown up with in her mother's household, Frances Stuart, was to journey to England to become the new queen's maid of honour. Without knowing that she would come to feature far more in her brother's life, Henrietta wrote 'I would not miss this opportunity of writing to you by Madame Stuart who is taking her daughter to be one of the maids of the Queen you wife. Had it not been for this purpose, I assure you I should have been very sorry to let her go from here, for she is the prettiest girl imaginable and the most fitted to adorn a Court'.[1]

Henrietta was soon bored of staying in bed at the Tuileries now she was Madame, Duchess d'Orleans, and a lauded lady at the French court so she reclined on a couch in her apartments and visitors came to amuse her from morning till night. Seeing as she had missed a court performance of a new ballet, the King, Queen and Philippe performed it for her in her rooms. The Comte de Guiche also appeared.

Henrietta had refused to receive him and returned his letters unopened for propriety's sake but she secretly enjoyed their flirtation. The king no longer paid her much attention and it was nice to know that someone else was enamoured of her. When de Guiche disguised himself as a fortune teller to come to her rooms, no one recognised him except the duchess. Her maid,

Anne-Constance de Montalais, brought her his letters and this time she read them. He brought amusement to her on the dullest of days.

Louise de La Valliere, the maid she had presented to Louis was now deeply in love with the king and he returned her affection. He regularly visited her on the pretext of seeing Henrietta Anne and not only did it annoy her, the Queen still thought his affection was for his sister-in-law. Henrietta asked Louise to leave to avert any further scandal and the scared young girl left in the night for a convent near Saint-Cloud but Louis was distraught and finding her gone rode out to bring her back. Returning her to the Tuileries he begged Henrietta to allow her to stay in her service and knowing everything about her flirtation the king promised to not banish de Guiche for his continued advances. Henrietta Anne agreed but told the king Louise was no longer her maid but his property – 'une fille-à-vous'.

By the second week of March Henrietta was well enough to appear in public, visiting her mother at the Palais-Royal and attending a thanksgiving service at Val-de-Grâce. She waited on Queen Marie-Therese at an audience with the Spanish ambassador but by now she was heavily pregnant. Earlier than expected she gave birth on 27 March to a daughter named Marie Louise. It was rumoured that on hearing she had had a girl, Henrietta told her maid to throw it in the river! It doesn't seem like her but women at the time longed for sons as heirs and this baby could possibly have been the king's.

There is no evidence that Henrietta actually slept with Louis but all the signs pointed to their relationship being that close. Henrietta had written to Charles that she had not slept with her husband on her wedding night as she had her period and that Philippe had difficulty consummating their marriage. These Stuart siblings really did like to share their secrets. Louis and Henrietta had spent the summer after her wedding together and would have had ample opportunity to take their relationship further. Although we will never know for sure this first daughter would be taken under the wing of the French queen dowager, her grandmother, who was devoted to her and raised in her household. She would also be the main beneficiary of Queen Anne's will.

Henrietta's admirer, the Comte de Guiche, left court at this time to join the army. The maid Montalais aided him in seeking a private audience with his beloved before he left but nothing was ever secret for long in the French court and Queen Anne soon found out. Montalais was sacked and Henrietta received a severe telling off from her mother whilst Philippe demanded an explanation. She told him everything. Their flirtation had been harmless and Philippe who had his own secrets was happy to let it go.

As the summer months passed Henrietta was back in full health and attending the entertainments. After the christening of her daughter in May a tournament was held and on 1 June the famous 'carrousel' was performed with knights dressed in costumes from around the world for a fantastic horsemanship display. She joined Louis at the stag hunt in Versailles in July leading the ladies on horseback and spent much time in the company of her mother at Colombes or Saint-Cloud.

The queen dowager left for England on 25 July and this time Henrietta Anne could not go with her. Charles had married Catherine of Braganza in May and the queen dowager wanted to spend time with her son and new bride. Charles was having difficulties as Henrietta had had. There was no sign of an heir yet and Catherine who had lived a sheltered life in Portugal had just found out about his long-term mistress Barbara Castlemaine who Charles demanded she make one of her ladies.

Henrietta wrote to him:

You tell me that some one has spoken ill of a certain person [Castlemaine] to the Queen your wife. Alas is it possible that such things are really said? I who know your innocence can only wonder! But to speak seriously, I beg you to tell me how the Queen has taken this. Here people say that she is in the deepest distress, and to speak frankly I think she has only too good reason for her grief.[2]

Henrietta had troubles of her own. She could barely tolerate her husband and with de Guiche gone, she encouraged a flirtation with the Marquis de Vardes, First Gentleman of the Bedchamber, but when she would not become his mistress his attentions became poisonous and he began to denigrate her, insinuating to the king she was not to be trusted. Henrietta's relationship with Louis had never fully recovered after the de La Valliere affair and Vardes just stirred the waters.

But Charles wished her to act as negotiator between himself and Louis to strengthen the ties between their two countries. He sent Ralph Montagu to her in October with a letter for herself and one written in French to be shown to Louis.

I avail myself of the permission which you have given me, to assure you of the continuation of those sentiments which you approve, and of my intentions to employ all the means that are the most likely to attain the fulfilment of our wishes. Nothing can better serve this end, than a close friendship between the King, my brother, and myself, and I assure you that this consideration was my chief reason in making this last Treaty, for an intimate alliance between us. In this I am persuaded that we shall have the advantage of your intervention, and if you think fit to propose that we should communicate our thoughts to each other through you, I shall be very glad, knowing how much this mutual confidence will assist in promoting our friendship. I have desired this bearer to inform you and the King, my brother, of the present state of affairs, and the object I pursue. He will assure you of all the imaginable respect which I cherish for your person, and my wish that you should become the witness and mutual pledge of the friendship that binds me to the King, my brother.[3]

It was the beginning of a more significant role for Henrietta between the two kings.

The Queen of France gave birth to a daughter Anne Elizabeth on 18 November but the baby died just six weeks later. The court continued its Christmas celebrations regardless. On Twelfth Night Moliere's *L'Ecole des Femmes* was performed at the Palais-Royal and dedicated to Henrietta. She was in charge of costumes and the production of the *Ballet des Arts* on 8 January with music by Lully and gave a masked ball at the end of the month. Ralph Montagu reported back to Charles on all the festivities prompting her brother to joke that here was another man in love with her.

The spring brought unhappiness for Henrietta when she miscarried the child she was carrying. Although relations with her husband were fraught this would definitely have been his child. It appeared that on occasion Philippe could carry out his marital duty. It was imperative that they had an heir for if Louis' children failed to thrive, theirs would be next in the succession.

Charles wrote to Henrietta of his eldest illegitimate son's marriage in April. James Crofts, created Duke of Monmouth, married Anne Scott, Countess of Buccleuch. As they were both so young, he fourteen, she twelve, Charles wrote 'we intend to dance and see them abed together, but the ceremony shall stop there, for they are both too young to be all night together'.[4]

Apart from his merriments Charles was becoming increasingly concerned with the French ambassador and did not hold much faith in the English Lord Holles either. In May he wrote:

I hope you have, before this, fully satisfied the King my brother of the sincerity of my desire to make a strict alliance with him, but I must deal freely with you, in telling you that I do not think his ambassador here, Monsieur de Cominges is very forward in the businesses. I cannot tell the reasons which make him so, but he finds upon occasions, so many difficultyes, as I cannot chuse but conclude, that we will not be able to advance much in this matter withhim, therefore I am hastening away my Lord Holles with all possible speede, to let the King my brother see that there shall nothing rest, on my parte, to the finishing that entier friendship I so much desire...[5]

Louis however was stricken with measles but as Henrietta Anne had already had them she was one of the very few who could visit him and thus their relationship began to improve. She assured him of her love for him and for France and rose again in his estimations.

The summer was spent at the Louvre rather than their customary sojourn into the countryside as the queen mother was ill. Instead Henrietta joined her husband and the king and queen on trips to Versailles and St-Cloud. Charles also sent her a barge richly decorated with blue velvet hangings embroidered with gold that became a favourite with the queen and queen mother when she recovered. It could be sailed along the Seine relieving the stuffiness of the court and was the focus of many a water party. One day when Henrietta took a trip up to Saint-Cloud with her husband she met some English men who she was delighted to take with her and show them her magnificent home and delightful gardens. It was an enjoyable day spent with Philippe and those were very few.

When he heard that Marsillac, the duc de la Rochefoucauld's eldest son, had fallen in love with his wife, as many of the young gallants did, he flew into a jealous rage so bad that Marsillac was forced to leave court. Then Philippe decided that the wife of his friend the Comte d'Armagnac should become one of her ladies. Henrietta, knowing the Comte also had feeling for her, refused seeing the trouble that lay ahead but it was brewing already. Madame d'Armagnac spurred on by troublemaker

Madame de Montespan placed the blame on one of Henrietta's oldest friends, Madame de Châtillon, affectionately known as Bablon. Philippe banned her from seeing Henrietta and in return Henrietta banned Madames d'Armagnac and de Montespan but she also told Louis of her troubles and Philippe was once more angrily put in his place.

Charles who was having his own troubles with a dangerously sick wife wrote:

> *Mr Montagu did shew me your letter concerning the businesse you had about Madame de Chatillon, and without being partiall to you, the blame was very much on the other side. I was very glad that the King tooke your parte, which in justice he could not do lesse...*[6]

Catherine of Braganza had been severely ill but Charles had devotedly tended her through her worst days even though he went back to his mistresses at night. In November he asked Henrietta to send her some pious pictures to cheer her bedchamber walls which she duly did.

At the start of a new year Moliere's new play *Le Mariage Forcé* was performed at the Louvre and Henrietta Anne was so impressed she asked for it to be enacted again at her house a month later. Henrietta enjoyed Moliere's work and was fast becoming a patron of the playwright standing as a sponsor for his son Louis named after the king. Moliere was more than a little enamoured of the duchess and in the dedication of his play *L'Ecole des Femmes* he wrote to her 'You are respected by all the world for your ran and birth. You are admired by all who see you for your graces of mind and person. Your soul is yet more beautiful, and if we may venture to say so, inspires all who have the honour of approaching you with love'.[7]

The *Ballets des Amours Deguisés* was performed at the Palais-Royal with the king, queen and Philippe taking key roles early in February but Henrietta, who was pregnant again, was too ill to join in. She rallied to attend the queen mother's ball at the Louvre during carnival week but took an unfortunate tumble when she tripped over one of the long ribbons hanging from her dress. Due to her condition she was proscribed bed rest for nine days and once recovered set out on her barge with the queen mother for Saint-Cloud before joining the court at the end of May in Fontainebleau. Louis held a week-long fete for the opening of his spectacular gardens at Versailles at the beginning of May held in honour of the queen and queen mother but in reality for his mistress Louise. Henrietta does not appear to have attended. She was still recovering both from her illness and the longevity of the king's favour towards the girl who had once been her maid.

Henrietta Anne found that all was not well here with Lord Holles, the English ambassador, who was stirring up trouble instead of looking after her brother's interests. He had taken slight at not being addressed as 'Your Excellency'. England was fast approaching open hostilities with the Dutch and Charles wrote to her in June that he had been inspecting his ships. They also discussed the East India Trading company whom Henrietta had invested in on behalf of her daughter, Marie Louise. Whilst Charles kept his sister abreast of the political situation, Holles was fast becoming a thorn in her side.

She had not time for him now as she took to her bed for the birth of Philippe Charles, duc de Valois, on 16 July, three weeks later than expected. Philippe sent his man Boyer with a note to Charles to tell him the good news of her safe delivery and Louis wrote to congratulate him:

We have this morning received the accomplishment of our wishes in the birth of a son, whom it has pleased God to give to my brother; and, to render this blessing complete in all points, nothing can be more favour able than the state of health, both of mother and child. With all my heart I congratulate your majesty; to understand my joy, you need only be pleased to estimate it by the greatness of your own, for my tenderness towards my brother and sister is not less than even that of your majesty.[8]

Henrietta needed to recover after this birth and it was a month before she was back at court. But during this time Vardes asked for an audience with her. She was forewarned of his intentions by the Comtesse de Soissons who knew of his meddling and blackening of Henrietta's name with Louis and Philippe. Vardes had heard de Guiche was back from the army and tried to catch her out by pretending to have a letter from him. She had agreed with Louis that she would not contact de Guiche nor receive any correspondence from him. Vardes wanted her to take the letter to prove her disloyalty to the king but Henrietta would have none of it and dismissed the man then told Louis all.

In August Henrietta Anne accompanied the king and queen to Vincennes whilst Philippe stayed at the Palais-Royal with the children. Holles writes of her as being 'grown so fat'[9] but given she was always thin, we can take this to just mean she was looking healthier. She joined her husband at Villers-Cotterêts but was by this time back to being 'slender and delicate'[10] and was prescribed a diet of asses milk to build her strength. It did the trick and Henrietta was well enough to organise a grand fete and a performance of Moliere's *Tartuffe* for the king and queen.

Her renewed strength led her to remonstrate with Charles regarding his political ambition. As anti-Dutch feeling was growing, Charles wanted France's allegiance. A previous treaty however acknowledged that France would assist Holland in times of war. Charles desperately wanted Henrietta to negotiate with Louis for an assurance that France would take England's side or stay out of any hostilities altogether. Henrietta put the blame on the failure of an alliance so far on the English and French ambassadors to which Charles wrote an indignant long reply where he reminded her of her English roots by referring to her as an Exeter woman and saying 'if you are not fully informed of all things as you complayne in your letters, it is your own faute, for I have been a very exact correspondent...'[11]

The siblings never fell out for too long. Henrietta Anne now became the principal negotiator between her brother and Louis and spoke to the king about an official treaty. Louis was happy enough to discuss it and referred her to a treaty he had signed back in 1644, ratifying a previous treaty of 1610. Henrietta had to send Charles a copy but he felt they would have to write and agree to new terms. His sister would have her work cut out for her.

In October Henrietta Anne moved to Versailles, the hunting lodge of Louis' father, which he would turn into the most magnificent palace. Here she wrote to Charles about some English jewels that had been found.

I have always delayed to mention to you a discovery which I made six months ago, of certain jewels, which are pretended to have been stolen from the king our father, and I should not now have written to you about it, but the ambassador, who was lately informed of it, will doubtless have done so already; and this being the case, as I can no longer give you the surprise I hoped for, I will tell you that the persons concerned in it, whom I have had imprisoned, confess to having had the jewels, but as they are a little scattered abroad, there will be some trouble in getting them again; but even should it cost more than trouble, they shall not escape me, that I may have the pleasure of restoring them to you. It is said that there are a hat-band of diamonds, very handsome, a garter also, and many rings; a portrait of Prince Henry as a child, set in very large diamonds. You can ascertain from the queen whether she knew them, for the king had nothing that she was unacquainted with.[12]

For the time being she was caught up in personal matters. A heavily pregnant Queen Marie-Therese was ill with fever and Henrietta helped care for her. She gave birth to her daughter prematurely but it was reported by Holles that the child was the colour of a 'blackamoor'. La Grande Mademoiselle did concur that the baby was very dark and rumours abounded that Louis was not the father and that it was the queen's African dwarf. There were also whispers that the child had been given to nuns to raise but the official version was that the child died four weeks after birth. It was yet another scandal for the gossips at the French court to relish.

The queen was not highly regarded. She had found it hard to fit in with the French court and Louis was not keen on her company finding her dull and boring. As so many other queens and princesses before her, she was just the means to an heir. The Archbishop of Sens described her:

> The queen was a saintly princess but lacked the social graces, being often disagreeable, and possessing none of the gentle arts that win a husband's heart. She too often displayed jealousy, and invariably failed to pay him those delicate compliments which kings are accustomed to receive from flattering courtiers. Her piety led her to go to church at times when the king desired her company in some party of pleasure, and she preferred to live retired among her dogs and Spanish dwarves rather than please him by taking part in the fetes and other diversions with which he entertained his court.[13]

In November Louis sent his envoy, the Marquis de Ruvigny, over to Charles. Henrietta asked him to take a letter to her brother in which she tells him how Louis wished for an accord.

> In God's name take advantage of this and do not lose any time in obtaining the King's secret promise that he will not help the Dutch for you understand he cannot promise you this openly because of his engagements with them...[14]

Henrietta Anne's relationship with Louis was in excellent form and it would stand her in good stead for what was to happen next. Although Henrietta had cut off all communication with de Guiche he managed to speak to her at a masked ball given by the Duchess de la Vieuville where his disguise foiled others from learning his identity. He told her of the lies Vardes had been spreading and the full extent of his plans to bring her down.

And he hadn't stopped yet. Vardes was busy denigrating Henrietta to the Chevalier de Lorriane who was in love with one of her ladies. Joking with him, he loudly said that Lorraine shouldn't bother with the maid when he could have the mistress instead. When Henrietta heard this latest slander she rushed to Louis and begged that Vardes be punished once and for all.

Henrietta feared what this latest outrage would do to her reputation and she begged Charles for help too.

Here I will say that the thing is so serious, I feel that it will influence the rest of my life. If I cannot obtain my object, it will be a disgrace to feel that a private individual has been able to insult me with impunity, and if I do, it will be a warning to all the world in future, how they dare attack me. I know that you were angry that he was not punished for the first affair, which makes me ask you this time to write a letter to the King, saying that although you feel sure he will give me every possible satisfaction, and finish as well as he has begun – for it will never do for us to let him see that we are displeased with him – yet, out of love for me you cannot help asking him to do so (if you do not think this expression too strong).[15]

Charles promised his assistance but there was not much he could do. It is not known if he did write to Louis about his sister's honour. Louis anyway had Vardes sent to the Bastille but even there he slandered Henrietta saying she had no real power and could never have him banished. Louis then did just that and sent him to Aigues-Mortes and forbid him to return to court. The Comtesse de Soissons who feeling much better by now and wanting her revenge on Henrietta for Vardes banishment told the King that she was planning to take Dunkirk in Charles' name and yet again Henrietta was forced to strongly deny the rumours. Louis had no intention of believing them and the Comte and Contesse were also banished from court and Vardes was further removed to the prison in Montpelier.

Henrietta was much more guarded now and was wary of who to trust and who to share confidences with. She had experienced first-hand how the court could turn against her and how easy it was for rumours to spread. Madame de Motteville wrote:

> The author of all these intrigues being removed, and without hope of return, Madame seemed to wish to change her conduct: she lived on better terms with the queen her mother-in-law, and seemed only to think of diversion that she might share with the king those fitting pleasures of a court which are deemed necessary, and that she might please all in general. As she had much genius and penetration, and talked sensibly on all subjects, those who had the honour of approaching her then, believed that there were moments in which, from her own experience, she had almost discovered that the charms of the life which she sought with so much eagerness, are not capable of satisfying the human heart; but she was not yet in a state fully to know that truth; she now saw it from afar, and athwart so many clouds, that it was impossible for her to be entirely influenced by it.[16]

De Guiche tried one more time to see her before he returned to war. Disguising himself as a servant he approached her as she was carried in a sedan chair from the Palais-Royal to the Louvre but he collapsed and was taken back to the Palais. Henrietta would never see him again.

In her memoirs, the later Duchesse d'Orleans wrote of Henrietta at that time as having 'more misfortunes than faults. She had to do with wicked people... Madame was very young, beautiful, agreeable, full of grace and charm. From the time of her marriage, she was surrounded by the greatest coquettes and most intriguing women in the world, who were the mistresses of her enemies. I think people have been very unjust to her'.[17]

Henrietta Anne turned her attention away from the ladies and their scandals and became more involved in intellectual pursuits. The Captain of the Musketeers and a Greek scholar, Monsieur de Treville, became a close acquaintance as did General Turenne, the renowned soldier, and she continued to show her patronage to the arts with her friendships with Moliere, La Fontaine and Racine. These were people she could really talk to and delight in their company rather than the gossips at court.

George Villiers, Duke of Buckingham

Chapter Seven

The Displeasure of a King

1665–1666

Henrietta Anne felt ill throughout the early months of 1665. Louis had asked her to organise a ballet, *La Naissance de Venus*, in which she played Venus. She felt extremely tired and struggled to put on the performance. Despite courtiers commenting on her thinness, she was in fact pregnant again and suffering through the early stages.

But it didn't stop her from corresponding with her brother in England and keeping abreast of recent political upheaval. There had been rumours about what was happening in Guinea. Charles had sent his captain, Holmes, to protect his interests there and the English had taken the fort at Cape Verde, seizing Dutch trading ships. Charles knew that Louis would be appalled and hesitant to further any treaty if it were the English who were the main aggressors. He promptly declared that Holmes had acted without his permission and he was thrown in to the Tower on his return. The English spread rumours that the Dutch were committing acts of cruelty and they had been forced to react. When Dutch ships began to fire on English warships in January Charles received support from parliament to the tune of £2,500,000 and on 4 March war was declared on Holland.

Louis was hedging his bets. France was Holland's ally but his father-in-law King Philip IV of Spain was dying which meant the French king could lay claim to Flanders, currently a Spanish territory, on behalf of his wife. Henrietta Anne was uncertain which way Louis would turn and she wrote to Charles to consider a secret treaty where he could pledge to help Louis thus gaining his support. But she was also wary of those around her and told

Charles 'My enemies here look so suspiciously on all I do, that soon I shall hardly venture to speak of your affairs!' and in her next correspondence tells him that their letters are often opened.

Henrietta was also fearful for her brother James, Duke of York, who had sailed with the English fleet to engage the Dutch. When the Battle of Lowestoft commenced, she received reports that James had died which sent her into a sudden and terrible decline. Further information filtering through told her in fact of the English victory and that James was safe and well. It was the Dutch flagship that had blown to smithereens with its admiral on board. But there had been many losses including that of their mutual friend Charles Berkeley and when Charles wrote to his Minette it was obvious he took no pleasure in the victory and was heavily mourning Berkeley's loss. Still he managed to tell her 'this great successe does not at all change my inclinations towards France, which you may assure the K., my brother, from me, and that it shall be his faute if we be not very good frindes'.[1]

Charles was entering a significantly troubled period in his reign. The plague had arrived in London carried by rat fleas and was spreading rapidly throughout the population. The king's mother, Henrietta Maria, made preparations to leave England and the disease behind and return to France. Her daughter was anxiously awaiting her and whilst she waited she penned a long letter to Charles urging him to be happy with his victory and to end hostilities with the Dutch now. She urged him to look for peace and told him that it was also the opinion of all at the French court that the war should end.

Henrietta was worn out and took to her bed where she gave birth to a daughter prematurely. The child did not survive and was quietly buried at Saint-Denis. Her mother had arrived and gave her comfort until she was well enough to leave for Colombes to spend the rest of the summer. The queen mother had been diagnosed with breast cancer and Louis had been told it was fatal. It cast a disquieting pall across the usually festive court.

Charles didn't want to add to Henrietta's unhappiness but he felt that she may be caught between himself and Louis as their relationship and that of their countries deteriorated. He wrote to her regardless explaining his fears and assuring her of his love and affection. His concern was only for his sister who would be placed in an uncomfortable position should the relationship between England and France worsen. King Louis was very aware that the situation was degrading. He visited Henrietta and her mother at Colombes. Holles had not been asked to the meeting but reported of it afterwards:

> The King of France and the Queen-mother went alone into her bed-chamber, and our Princess, Madame, went in, after they had been there at least an hour. When the King of France went away, I had an interview with the Queen-mother afterwards, and took the boldness to ask her how she found things. She said, they had been all the time within talking over these businesses of Holland, and that Louis XIV. Told her he had made King Charles some propositions, which were very fair ones, which, if he refused, he must take part with the Hollanders.[2]

The political atmosphere was a heavy one but where would the French court be without its gaiety and splendour? Henrietta invited the court to Villers-Cotterêts in September for hunting, balls and plays and more of the same took place at Christmas. Henrietta and her husband held a ball at the Palais-Royal, Moliere's *Medicin Malgré Lui* was performed and there was further festivities for the wedding of Henrietta's maid, Mademosielle d'Artigny. Only this time the queen was absent from the celebrations due to her father King Philip's demise and neither was the queen mother whose health was rapidly deteriorating.

Although Henrietta had long been disillusioned with her

husband, she was with him after Anne of Austria drew her final breath. They withdrew to Saint-Cloud whilst funeral arrangements were made and returned to be chief mourners with Henrietta wearing a train, seven yards long, for the proceedings. The queen mother had left her several of her fabulous jewels but it was to her daughter Marie Louise that she left her fortune.

The King of France did not attend. The English parliament had discussed Louis' proposals and rejected them. A week after his mother was buried, Louis declared war on England. Charles wrote to Henrietta warning her that their correspondence would probably become more difficult now and there are far less letters extant for the next two years. Henrietta keenly felt the loss of her brother's constant correspondence and to make matters worse now Louis was upset with her.

Louis had continued his relationship with Louise de la Vallière who was pregnant again. She had already given birth to three of the king's sons yet none had survived infancy. The queen who surely knew but had ignored this now decided to put her foot down and ordered her dismissal. Or was fed up with it being flaunted in her face and annoyed that this pregnant lady was so obviously unmarried and a mistress of the king. Either way Henrietta agreed with her and Louis was furious. Wasn't it her fault that he had been thrown together with Louise anyway? Louise quietly retired to await the birth of her daughter who would be born later in the year and grow up to be the Princess de Conti.

Henrietta felt utterly friendless and the following months would only add to her unhappiness. Her home life was uncomfortable to say the least. Philippe had taken up with the Chevalier de Lorraine, who had previously chased her maid and now became her husband's intimate lover. His influence over Philippe was frightening and as their affair progressed Lorraine came to dominate Henrietta's husband and cause her much pain.

Although she had not heard from Charles since May, news

reached her of the Great Fire of London in September which horrified and appalled her, but at least Charles and James were safe. They had helped to fight the blaze that had engulfed the capital city for nearly a week and in a letter she received from Charles in November he was back to discussing peace negotiations with Louis as if nothing had happened.

One man who became her close confidant at this time and was a soothing balm for her troubles was Daniel de Cosnac, the Bishop of Valence and the Grand Almoner of Philippe's household. A pamphlet had been written about her supposed amours with de Guiche which was published in Holland. Cosnac sent his man to buy up all the copies, 1800 of them, and obtain an order prohibiting further publication. They were duly delivered to her and burnt in front of her. If Philippe had seen them he would have been enraged and with Lorraine beside him Henrietta dreaded what they would do. Cosnac would forever remain in her favour after his kind act. He would later say 'The whole affair cost me a great deal of trouble and money, but, far from regretting this, I was only too well paid by the thanks which Madame bestowed upon me'.[3]

Henrietta was rehearsing for her performance in Molière's *Ballet des Muses* in November when she heard that her son was ill. He was at Saint-Cloud with his nurse when he developed a high fever. Henrietta rushed to him but found little Philippe on the mend so she took him back to Paris with her where he was pronounced well by her doctor. He was housed at the Palais-Royal whilst she left for St-Germain to appear in the ballet in front of the court but the very day after her performance she was recalled to Paris. Philippe had relapsed and was having convulsions. Not yet christened, Cosnac was asked to conduct the ceremony. Although there was a brief ceremony after a child was born, French royalty were usually baptised at the age of twelve.

Philippe died the next day. It was a huge loss to Henrietta but also to the royal family as a whole. Louis' own son, the Dauphin, was a sickly child and they had hoped that at least little Philippe would thrive. His funeral was attended by hundreds of people who mourned the loss of a Prince of the Blood. Cosnac officiated delivering a beautiful sermon that brought tears to everyone's eyes but helped to relieve Henrietta's sorrow.

There is no evidence that she wrote to her brother but this poignant death healed the rift between herself and Louis. The king wrote to inform Charles of the tragic news:

The common loss we have had at the death of my nephew the Duc de Valois touches us both so closely that the only difference in our mutual grief is that mine began a few days sooner than yours.[4]

Chapter Eight

Troubled Days

1667–1668

Henrietta was not allowed to mourn for too long. Louis would never cancel his ongoing celebrations, festivities and entertainments – not even for the death of his nephew. Instead of being callous he showed a stoic resolve to continue on in the face of adversity and so he asked her to perform again in Molière's ballet as a shepherdess with her little spaniel, Mimi, on 12 January 1667 at the Palais-Royal. There was a new royal baby too for the queen had given birth to daughter. It meant the queen was indisposed and Henrietta was called upon to once again take her place at Louis' side.

Their renewed relationship came at a time of reinvigorated peace talks with England. Louis had no real need to continue a war with the English but had been forced to support the Dutch as his allies. Now he wanted to take Flanders and the Dutch refused to recognise his sovereignty. He could break their alliance and once more treat with Charles.

Henrietta had been a part of ongoing negotiations but her mother had also been playing a prominent role in promoting Charles' interests. In April a secret treaty was delivered to the queen dowager at Colombes. A meeting would be held at Breda in the summer to ratify its conditions.

The French army headed by Turenne marched with 50,000 men towards Flanders. In May, Louis joined them as did Philippe who dramatically told Henrietta she might never see him again. It is hard to think she would be too sorrowed by the thought. She was pregnant again and unwell. At St-Cloud, she heard news of the campaign as it progressed. Cosnac had also joined the fray and she awaited reports daily. Philippe appeared to be thriving as a military man although he soon got bored and spent more time in his sumptuously decorated tent. When Henrietta miscarried another child he returned home to her to find her severely ill.

Philippe wrote to Charles:

Madame begs me to ask Your Majesty's pardon for not writing by this post, but she has not the strength to sit up, since the accident which happened to her a week ago, after which she was thought to be dead during a quarter-of-an-hour. This has obliged me to leave Douay, before the entrance of the King, my brother, to whose arms the town surrendered three hours before my departure.[1]

Louis also paid her a visit. He was taking a break at Compiegne with the queen and his ladies. Louise de la Valliere was back having been made a duchess but Louis' eyes had turned to a new mistress, Athénaïs, Marquise de Montespan, maid of honour to Queen Marie-Therese. Before long the king and Philippe returned to the war which was more of a triumphal progress as a contemporary wrote 'the streets are full of cloth of gold, of waving plumes, of chariots and superbly-harnessed mules, of horses with gold and embroidered trappings, and of sumptuous carriages'.[2] Even when Louis went to war he did it in style.

After the surrender of Lille, the royals returned home leaving the war to their accomplished general Turenne. Philippe went to his wife at Villers- Cotterêts where she was recuperating with her mother. Before long the Chevalier de Lorraine joined him, he was given the best of apartments at the Palais-Royal and rarely left the duke's side. Henrietta spoke to Cosnac of her concern over her husband's behaviour. Philippe in turn grew jealous of Henrietta's relationship with the Bishop and paranoid of their conversations. Although Henrietta remonstrated with her husband telling him that Cosnac's only fault was to serve him with too much zeal and loyalty, the bishop had been made to feel too uncomfortable to stay and took his leave.

Lonely once more, Henrietta frequently visited her mother at Colombes and met up with her friend Madame de La Fayette who was writing the princess's memoirs with her when they could snatch quiet moments. It was here she heard of the Dutch raid on England. Charles had laid up the English fleet whilst peace talks were ongoing but the Dutch made one final attack before any treaty was signed. In June, they took the fort at Sheerness and sailed on up the Medway to burst through the chain protecting the entrance to the royal boatyard at Chatham. Charles' flagship, the *Royal Charles*, was captured as well as the *Unity* and the *Royal Oak*, *Royal James* and *Loyal London* plus other ships were set alight. When the Dutch withdrew they took the *Royal Charles* with them as a final humiliating act. However, the signing of the treaty of Breda still took place and was ratified by England, the United Provinces (Netherlands), France, and Denmark–Norway.

Someone had to take the blame. Charles dismissed his chancellor, the earl of Clarendon, but Henrietta Anne was appalled at the news. The man had loyally served their father as well as her brother. But the king was too caught up in his latest amours to discuss it with her. Charles was more concerned with writing of Frances Stuart who had grown up in Queen Henrietta Maria's French household and had been Henrietta Anne's childhood friend. She had become maid of honour to Queen Catherine where she came to the king's attention. Frances had flirted with the king but never wanted to take their relationship further. She was loyal to the queen and asked for her help to escape the court and the king's attentions. This she did by eloping with the Duke of Richmond and Charles was still smarting from the insult when he wrote:

... how hard a thing tis to swallow an injury done by a person I

had so much tendernesse for, you will in some degree excuse the resentment I use towards her; you know my good nature enough to believe that I could not be so severe, if I had not great provocation, and I assure you her carriage towards me has been as bad as breach of frindship and faith can make it, therefore I hope you will pardon me if I cannot so soon forget an injury which went so neere my hart.[3]

Henrietta Anne had little time for her brother's laments. She was pleased that Frances had made a suitable marriage rather than being the king of England's mistress. At least she was happy whereas Henrietta was finding it harder and harder to live with her husband's lover in her household. No wonder that in October she suffered from excruciating headaches and was so ill she couldn't even write to her brother. Philippe however did his duty and let him know:

Madame begs me to excuse her to you that she does not write, but for six days she has had headaches so violent that she has had her shutters closed. She has been bled in the foot, and has tried many other remedies, but they have not relieved her at all.[4]

Despite Henrietta Anne's protestations, Charles agreed that the earl of Clarendon could be impeached on seventeen charges but the chancellor's peers refused to accept the charges. Her brother wrote to Henrietta in November but still referred to the earl's ill conduct. Despite his years of loyalty, there would be no backing down. With rumours that Charles would convene a court to try him – a case that would result in his execution, the Earl of Clarendon fled to France at the end of the year, living in exile and moving from place to place. It was an unhappy end to such an illustrious career.

Henrietta Anne was also hoping for a better year to come as 1667 drew to a close. In November Racine had dedicated *Andromaque* to her with the words 'they may condemn my Andromaque as much as they will, now I can appeal from the subtleties of their imagining, to the heart of your Royal Highness. But, Madame, I know that you judge the merits of a work, not alone by the heart but by the light of an intellect that cannot be deceived'[5] and she continued to be a patron of the arts. Christmas would be a round of balls and masques. Her health had improved and she looked forward to the festivities made all the more exciting by the arrival of James, Duke of Monmouth, Charles' illegitimate son. It gave her an excuse to absorb herself in the organising of entertainments especially in his honour. She arranged for him to have a luxurious suite at the Palais-Royal for which Charles thanked her as well as her ability to dissuade him for the time being from joining the army. But even now Philippe, spurred on by Lorraine, tried to spoil her happiness, complaining that they spoke too much in English and that James took up too much of her time.

Charles new agreement with Holland and Sweden – the Triple Alliance signed in 1668 – had upset Louis. It allowed for France to keep its existing territories but to take no more. Louis who was still on campaign at least did not blame Henrietta Anne for her brother's actions. From Dijon, he wrote:

If I did not love you so well, I should not write to you, for I have nothing to say, and have given my brother all the news there is to tell. But I am very glad to be able to assure you once more of what I have already told you, which is that I have as much affection for you as you can possibly desire.[6]

By March Henrietta was ill again, this time with her stomach. She had told Charles that she would travel to Bourbon to take the waters but her brother was not convinced that her current doctor was good enough and he sent over his own doctor Alexander Fraizer who had treated Henrietta as a baby to help with 'those kinde of obstructions'. Charles instructed her to 'have a care of your diet and believe the planer your diet is the better health you will have. Above all have a care of strong brothes and gravy in the morning...'[7] Although it seems that her condition only improved after taking some pills invented by Sir Theodore Mayerne who had once treated her mother.

The Duke of Monmouth was recalled to England after his wife broke her thigh in an accident. Once her leg was set and she began healing, he returned to France. On his return in June Philippe's jealousy reared up again. Not only was he incensed with any friendships Henrietta Anne made, he also found out that his lover Lorraine was still sleeping with his wife's maid, Mademoiselle Fiennes. Philippe dismissed her without Henrietta's knowledge. Mystified she searched her maid's rooms and found a casket of letters between Fiennes and Lorraine that contained slanderous references to herself and Monsieur. Henrietta did not know who to trust with the information and so she turned to Cosnac who read through the letters and saw a chance in them to have Lorraine discredited. He took them to the king who although was despairing of Philippe saw no reason to get involved. Philippe however was furious and revoked Cosnac's position of Grand Almoner making him return to his diocese in disgrace. Yet again Henrietta lost her valued and trusted friend.

Louis had been forging ahead with his ambitious plans for Versailles and on the 18 July a fete was held like never before with magnificent fireworks, water displays and Moliere's new play, *Georges Dandin*, performed to show off the king's new lavish gardens. The fete was held officially to celebrate a new treaty with Spain and the Duke of Monmouth was the most honoured guest but secretly it was all for Louis' new mistress, Madame de Montespan.

The duke returned to England shortly after and took messages from Henrietta to her brother. His letters again refer to a more amicable relationship between himself and Louis. The

French king had sent a new ambassador to London, Colbert de Croissy, and was awaiting his arrival. In return Ralph Montagu was appointed ambassador in France and although he would not take up his position until spring 1669 Henrietta was looking forward to working with him to improve the relationship between England and France.

It also seems that Henrietta Anne was getting on better with her husband. Charles replied to a letter she wrote on her marital situation that he was 'glad that Monsieur begins to be ashamed of his ridiculous fancyes'.[8] Lorraine was the prime one of those and although Henrietta felt her situation was improving, he was someone who would not give up his position easily.

Charles following letters now earnestly begin to discuss a secret treaty. In September Henrietta wrote her longest letter to him outlining her view on current politics and the way forward as she saw it.

Following the promise I made to you to let you know my opinion and what I have been able to see in this important business I will tell you that the order into which the King has put his finances has greatly increased his power and has put him more than ever in a position to make attacks on his neighbours, but so long as England and Holland are united they have nothing to fear from that quarter, and they can even protect their neighbours as they have been seen to do at the time of the last war in Flanders, when they became allied because they were indirectly interested in the preservation of that country. It is not surprising then that the majority of people who do not know the inside of things judge that the safest part you can play would be not to enter into any alliance against Holland. But the matter takes on a different aspect, firstly because you have need of France to ensure the success of the design about R. (religion) and there is very little likelihood of your obtaining what you desire from the King except on condition that you enter into a league with him against Holland. I think you must take this resolution, and when

115

you have thought it well over you will find that besides the intention of R. your glory and your profit will coincide in this design. Indeed what is there more glorious and more profitable than to extend the confines of your kingdom beyond the sea and to become supreme in commerce, which is what your people most passionately desire and what will probably never occur so long as the Republic of Holland exists?

It is true that by establishing your dominion on the ruins of that of Holland you will also contribute towards increasing that of the King, who aspires perhaps not less than yourself to becoming supreme in commerce; but the situation of your Kingdom, the number, the extent, and the order of your ports which are suitable for the biggest vessels, the natural disposition of your subjects, and the convenience you possess for building vessels remarkable for the manner of their construction and their power of endurance are advantages which France cannot possess; and to these advantages you can add that of reserving yourself, in the division you will make, the most important maritime towns, whose commerce will depend entirely on the laws which you choose to impose upon them for the benefit of your kingdom and yourself. I know well that there are some people who think that after France has increased her power by bringing about the downfall of Holland she would endeavour to take away from you your share of the conquests you will have made; but besides the ease with which you could hold the towns near to you it is easy to see that this opinion is not well-founded when one considers that by the division of the conquests of the territories which the Dutch possess in Europe the King will become more than a near neighbour of Flanders and of several German states, which, as well as Spain, would have an interest in combining to take measures to assure you your conquests. For it is certain that after having deprived you of them France would not spare them; and it would even be in the King's own interests to remain allied to you, because if he should separate himself from you his conquests would be in greater danger than yours; since, judging from all appearance, he would have much trouble in finding anyone to form a league with him against you, and you would easily find amongst these neighbours, and amongst others as well, plenty disposed to join you against him. And as for the countries which the Dutch possess outside Europe, you could take and keep what you will have agreed to take as your share with all the more ease in that you already possess considerable settlements in various parts which are near to them. And so it appears that you should easily enough be able to make your Parliament agreeable to your alliance with France; and if you foresee that you cannot at first obtain from them all the money of which you are in need to fit yourself out for war, you can oblige the King to make you a considerable advance, which will serve as a pledge of the sincerity of his procedure. And when the war has begun your Parliament will take care not to let you want for what you will require for the successful outcome of an enterprise on which will depend not only the glory and profit but even the security of the whole Kingdom. This war is not likely to be of long duration if the right measures are taken, and far from injuring the design you have touching R. it will perhaps give you the means of executing it with greater certainty and ease. But if you wish to begin by the execution of this design you will perhaps encounter obstacles which will prevent you from being able to think of anything else and cause you to miss the opportunity of profiting by all the advantages that you can hope for in agreeing at once to what the King desires of you. Up to now I have only spoken of your interest joined to that of your kingdom; but it is easy to see that the execution of the design which is being proposed to you would be the veritable foundation of your own greatness, because, having a pretext for keeping up troops outside your kingdom to protect your conquests, the thought alone of these troops, which for greater safety could be composed of foreigners and would be practically in sight of England, could keep it in check and render Parliament more amenable than it has been accustomed to be.as for your design to oblige the King to be the first to declare himself against the Dutch, *it seems to me that since England has engaged herself to help them by the League of Defence she has made with them, it would not be so honest on your part to fail in this engagement and abandon them in order to ally yourself with France, as to break with them first yourself on any of those grounds which you agree can spring up any day out of the jealousy between the two nations and their commercial rivalry. If you should be the first to declare yourself it would not be necessary for you to begin the war save in conjunction with France who would declare immediately afterwards; but if France should declare herself first, and the English Parliament – on the conduct of which it is only possible to make very uncertain conjectures – were to insist on maintaining the defensive League between England and Holland and on granting money only on this condition, France would find herself engaged to make war without the help of England to whom this inconvenience could not happen if she declares herself first, because the execution of the King of France's will depends on himself alone. I think, therefore, that if it suits you to be the first to break with Holland, the two designs, that is to say that of R. and that of the Dutch war, could be executed at the same time. And you would find it in this advantage: that at the same time as the King sends you troops you could send him such as you judge suitable to do and give the command of them to persons whose presence in England might be embarrassing to you.*

So far as the Pope is concerned it seems to me that it would be useless and even dangerous to confide your design to him at the present moment; since he will have no part in it execution and there would be danger that the secret might be discovered. It is true that the present Pope is a man whose mind and intentions are very honourable; but he may perhaps not live until the time when he will actually be needed; and there is a great likelihood that his successor, whoever he may be, will not fail to furnish every possible facility in order that his Pontificate may be honoured by the reconciliation of England to the Church of Rome.

I have become engaged in such a long discussion and my zeal has carried me so far that I no longer dare to direct this letter to you. I only venture to assure you that the same tenderness which leads me into arguments more serious than are becoming to me will always cause me to act in such a manner as to make you admit that there is no one who loves you as much as I.[9]

Henrietta Anne was an astute and intelligent woman who had always made it her goal to unite their countries; she would continue to make it her life's work. By return Charles suggested they start to use a cipher to keep their correspondence secret. The reason for such secrecy was that the English king knew how unpopular the treaty would be with his countrymen. Not only did he want to revive the Dutch war but he was also promising to convert to Catholicism. Something he had always fought against with regards to his siblings. Their brother James, however, had admitted he was Catholic and Henrietta had always been brought up in the faith. Charles' decision may have been a spiritual one but it was also political and it could not be made public just yet for fear of another civil war.

Whilst Henrietta Anne's correspondence with Charles stepped up a pace, another scandal threatened to rock her world. The Chevalier de Rohan had fallen in love with her and disgusted by the way in which Lorriane treated his lover's wife, he struck Philippe's paramour in public and called him to a duel. Henrietta had done nothing to encourage Rohan and asked the king to intervene to stop any bloodshed. Louis had the chevalier reprimanded and the scandal was averted.

Henrietta was now pregnant again and Charles wasn't overly pleased saying 'I must confesse, I would rather have had you stayd some monthes before you had been with childe'.[10] He unsympathetically saw her as his key negotiator and could only see a delay in the pushing forward of a treaty with his sister indisposed.

Chapter Nine

A Hateful Husband

1669–1670

The year 1669 started with more pressing correspondence from Charles using the cipher they had discussed. His councillors had suspicions he was secretly negotiating with the French and Charles reminded Henrietta Anne especially not to mention anything to the Duke of Buckingham. Buckingham was one of his favourites but the man was troublesome. He was constantly conspiring in some intrigue and was no friend to Charles' wife, Queen Catherine, even conspiring to have her kidnapped and shipped abroad. Neither had he been a friend to the earl of Clarendon, being instrumental in his downfall. Now he was part of the 'Cabal' who advised Charles: Clifford, Arlington, Buckingham, Ashley and Lauderdale. Charles encouraged Henrietta Anne to write to Buckingham and Arlington to discuss the prospects of England and France but to never discuss their true intentions. The king was happy with her role telling her in June that he had seen her letter to the duke and 'what you write to him is as it ought to be'.[1] It was one of the final letters that exist between the siblings. Due to the sensitivity of their letters it is possible that any others were destroyed. We know that she continued to work towards the treaty with Louis writing of her as 'the intermediary of this negotiation, as she is herself so natural a bond of union between us'.[2]

By June Henrietta was at Saint-Cloud facing the third trimester of her pregnancy. She had been so unwell with it that she had hardly seen her mother whose health was also poor. She received news from the court that Queen Marie-Therese was safely delivered of a son on 2 August and she hoped too that she would have a son to fill the gap her precious Philippe had left. Queen dowager Henrietta Maria managed to visit her daughter on the 23rd but was too ill to return when her daughter gave birth four days later. It was a girl who she named Anne Marie but she was severely disappointed and fell into a depression which was only made worse when she heard the news that her dearest mother had passed away at Colombes.

For months the once queen had been feeling unwell with pains in her side and acute insomnia. Her doctor, Monsieur Vallot, also physician to the king suggested she take a sedative, three grains of opium, to help her sleep. Henrietta Maria at first refused saying 'An astrologer told me, years ago, in England, a grain would be the cause of my death, and I fear M. Vallot's grain may be that fatal grain'.[3] She was finally convinced to take the dose to get some rest. She never woke up.

Louis ordered a state funeral for her at the Basilica of Saint-Denis in Paris. The Abbé Bossuet's sermon was magnificent and as well as praising the life of the queen mother he reminded the gathered crowd of Henrietta's escape from England and asked for her protection now.

Princess, whose future destiny is to be so great and glorious! Must you be born in the power of the enemies of your race? Eternal God! Watch over her! Holy angels, surround her with your unseen squadrons, and guard this illustrious and forsaken child. God did protect her, messieurs! Her governess, two years afterwards, saved her precious charge from the hands of the rebels, and although conscious of her own greatness, the child revealed herself, and refusing all other names, insisted on calling herself the princess, she was safely borne to the arms of her royal mother, to be her consolation in misfortune, and to become the happy spouse of a great prince, and the joy of all France.[4]

As she would have wished, Henrietta Maria's heart was placed in a silver casket and interred in her convent in Chaillot.

Philippe claimed that since she had died without a will all her possessions should come to himself and his wife as she was her only child in France. Henrietta Anne objected knowing that under English law Charles was his mother's heir and that many of her possessions had belonged to their father, Charles I, and should be returned to England. In November, the king asked for an inventory of the queen mother's effects. He agreed that Colombes should become Henrietta Anne's and that the nuns at Chaillot should have the furniture there that belonged to the queen. Paintings and jewellery were shipped back to England except Henrietta's favourite pearls that also went to her daughter.

Henrietta Anne was devastated by her mother's death. Her husband had joined Louis at Chambord whilst she preferred to remain at Saint-Cloud. Her brother, the Duke of York, had sent his daughter Anne to join his mother's household whilst she was receiving treatment for her eyes and Henrietta now took her into her own nursery to be raised with her children. She had to put up with many callers who offered their condolences and although well-meaning tired her with their incessant visits. She was however delighted when her old friend Madame de La Fayette arrived and convinced her to continue with her memoirs to take her mind off the present and delve back into the past. Henrietta spent many hours with her talking of better times whilst de La Fayette wrote down all she heard. The Abbé Bossuet also became a regular caller and they formed a solid friendship discussing religious matters long into the evenings.

She would have liked to talk to her old friend Cosnac who was still banished from court. Instead she wrote to him of how she had decided to use her influence to have him made a cardinal. Although she was sworn to secrecy over the treaty she also alluded to this being done through Charles when England became more important in the eyes of Rome. She took a risk writing such things down but she also talked to Cosnac of her marriage telling him 'I cannot bear to recognise his faults, although he has so many that by this time I ought to be used to it'.[5] Their letters were highly personal and shows how vulnerable she felt at the time.

Cosnac felt for her and decided he would try to see her arranging to meet at a friend's house in Saint-Denis but he became ill and had to hide at a lodging house. He sent his nephew to give important papers to Madame de Saint-Chaumont, a loyal member of Henrietta's household and governess to her children, to pass on to her mistress. His absence from his parish had been noted and he was found by the police, arrested and taken to the prison Fort d'Eveque and then exiled to L'Isle-Jourdain.

Henrietta Anne was mortified and worse was to come. The police had found a letter he had overlooked addressed to Madame de Saint-Chaumont and was suspicious of their correspondence. He sent Turenne to her with orders for the governess's dismissal. Henrietta had so few friends around her that to lose such a valuable woman was another devastating blow, made worse by her husband's lover crowing that he had been responsible for the loss of all her friends.

Charles was aware of Henrietta Anne's predicament through the reports of his ambassador. Ralph Montagu was appalled at her treatment and how depressed she had become. He wrote to Charles:

I would humbly propose to your Majesty what Madame had already discoursed me of, which is, that your Majesty would tell the French ambassador in England, that you know the Chevalier de Lorraine is the occasion of all the ill that your sister suffers, and that she is one that you are so tender of that you cannot think the French king your friend, whilst he suffers such a man about his brother, by whose counsels he doth every day so many things to Madame's dissatisfaction.[6]

When Charles received this letter he called for Croissy, the French ambassador, and made him well aware of his displeasure at his sister's situation. Communicating the king of England's feelings to Louis, he was assured that Lorraine would be dealt with.

Henrietta felt some hope when she wrote to Cosnac in December 'If the King keeps his promises which he daily repeats to me, I shall in future have less cause for annoyance, but you know how little I have learnt to trust such words...'[7]

Louis was waiting for an opportunity to bring Lorraine down and it came early in 1670 when Philippe asked the king to give the chevalier the revenues from two vacant abbeys. Louis refused – this was not the kind of man who deserved any benefices from the church. Philippe raged and swore he would leave court forever, flouncing off to find his lover to tell him the news. Lorraine reacted with words against the king and when Louis heard it, it gave him the chance to have Lorraine arrested and sent to Pierre-Encise, near Lyons.

Philippe fainted and when he recovered blamed Henrietta Anne for his lover's misfortune. As punishment, he ordered her to Villers-Cotterêts, a particularly cold place in winter. Before she left she wrote to Turenne:

> I only write to bid you farewell, for things have come to such a pass that, unless the King detains us by much affection and a little force, we go to-day to Villers-Cotterets, to return I know not when. You will understand what pain I feel from the step which Monsieur has taken, and how little compared with this I mind the weariness of the place, the unpleasantness of his company in his present mood, and a thousand other things of which I might complain. My only real cause of regret is having to leave my friends, and the fear I feel that the King may forget me.[8]

Philippe refused to return to court and Louis angered at his brother had Lorraine moved to Marseilles. As Henrietta Anne had written his mood was unpleasant and now he refused to sleep with her. That we may think would be a blessing for Henrietta but she was second lady of France and her duty was to produce male heirs. Philippe had never forgiven her for being high in his brother's favour and now it was her fault his lover was imprisoned. He would be as nasty as he liked and try to thwart her at every turn.

But she had one thing to look forward to and that was a trip to England. Montagu wrote previously of the possibility of Henrietta visiting her brother more as a respite from Lorraine than participating in Charles' actual plans. The ambassador does not seem to have been versed in the complexities of the treaty which the king of England thought could be brought over to him by his sister's own hand. Despite her personal troubles, the interests of England were of tantamount importance to her but she was shocked by Charles' excessive demands.

Charles had to lay out his intentions regarding England's naval force to Louis. In January 1670 he stated 'As a war against Holland would in all respects suit with the interests of England and be very advantageous to it if the King of Great Britain had force ready to be master of the seas; so on the other hand if the Hollanders should be strongest at sea nothing in the world could be so pernicious to England as that war'.[9]

Lord Falconbridge, ambassador to Venice, Florence and Savoy, was asked to take official letters of request to France for Henrietta Anne's visit on his journey south in February. Falconbridge sent his secretary, Doddington, to Henrietta at Villiers who reported that she was hoping to meet her brother at Dover when the court moved to Flanders. Letters had been written to her husband to ask for his permission but coming so soon after Lorraine's fall and his constant unpleasantness it had not deemed wise to ask him just yet.

Philippe was still smarting in February when he wrote to

Colbert de Croissy to tell his brother 'I am come here in an extremity of grief, at finding myself obliged to leave him, or to live at court with shame; that I entreat him to consider what the world would say if I were seen cheerful and tranquil amidst the pleasures of Saint-Germain and the carnival, whilst an innocent prince, the best friend I had in the world, and attached to me, lingers for my sake in a miserable prison, banished to a distance from me'.[10] Croissy visited to try to persuade Philippe back to court. His quarrel with his brother was now the talk of all the gossips but he refused.

Louis sent Henrietta Anne many gifts which she had apparently won at the annual lottery to try to cheer her up. Gloves, perfume, lace, jewellery and twenty purses of gold helped to lift Henrietta's spirits though angered her husband still further. As well many of the ladies at court wrote to her. Madame de Suze sent a note to one of her own ladies saying 'everyone here is very dull in Madame's absence, and unless she returns soon, I cannot think what we will do with ourselves. Nobody thinks of anything else but writing to her, and the ladies of the Court are to be seen, pen in hand at all hours of the day... She alone can bring us back the Spring-time'.[11]

The royal couple returned to court at the end of February. Louis had requested their presence and Philippe had bored of his tantrum and self-imposed exile. Many noted how pale and thin Henrietta Anne was and put it down to her recent troubles. They also noticed how badly Philippe treated his wife. La Grande Mademoiselle felt it her duty to remind her cousin that she was the mother of his children and he should show some respect. He was in a better mood due to Lorraine being freed but sent to Italy. Still he would never forgive Henrietta and never make any effort to see her happy. Henrietta is reported to have said 'If he had strangled me when he fancied that I had wronged him I could, at least, have understood it, but to go on teasing me like he does, all about nothing, this is really more than I can bear'.[12] Philippe was surrounding himself with other men that Henrietta despaired of and she wrote to her friend Madame de Saint-Chaumont:

> I see from the ashes of Monsieur's love for the Chevalier, as from the dragon's teeth, a whole brood of fresh favourites are likely to spring up to vex me. Monsieur now puts his trust in the little Marsan (another prince of the house of Lorraine) and the Chevalier de Beuvron, not to speak of the false face of the marquis de Villeroy, who prides himself on being his friend, and only seeks his own interests, regardless of those of Monsieur, or of the Chevalier.[13]

The one thing she could look forward to was her voyage to England. Louis felt the time was right to approach his brother on the subject of Henrietta Anne's trip. Philippe knew nothing of the treaty but had been informed by Lorraine of this proposal and raged at Louis that not only would he not let Henrietta go to see her brother, he would not even allow her to accompany the court to Flanders. How had he found out? It seems that Turenne had let slip to one of Henrietta's ladies who in turn had told Lorraine. As ever secrets were not kept for long in the French court but although it was now known amongst some that Henrietta may travel across the water, her true purpose was only known to a select few.

Finally Jean-Baptiste Colbert, the French minister of finance, convinced Philippe to allow her to travel to England. The duke relented but only on the condition he could go with her and only as far as Dover. This was ridiculous. How could Henrietta work on the treaty with her husband around who watched her every move? Charles used etiquette to dissuade him. If Philippe came to England then by rights the Duke of York should go to France, but this he was unable to do at the present time. Philippe mounted objection upon objection until Louis firmly told him that Henrietta must go for the good of the state. He acquiesced but stuck to their meeting being only of three days duration and she was not under any circumstances to travel to London. Philippe now had a change of tactic and slept with his wife every day to make her pregnant so she wouldn't be able to visit her brother. We can only imagine how reviled she must have been by his behaviour.

Henrietta Anne would join the court on their progress to Flanders but leave them at Dunkirk to take ship. Louis gave her 200,000 crowns to help with her preparations and expenses. Before she left she wanted her daughter Anne Marie, Mademoiselle de Valois, to be baptised and this was arranged for 8 April in the chapel at the Palais-Royal.

Philippe constantly aggravated her and wanted her to plead with the king for Lorraine's release which she refused to do. She asked Louis to at least allow her husband to give his lover pensions and gifts to keep him happy. Although Louis told her he would do nothing for Lorraine he told her husband that he would. Anything to keep Philippe appeased so that Henrietta could further the secret treaty.

Henrietta Anne was uncertain of the king's feelings towards Lorraine and dreaded such an outcome as his release. To Madame de Saint-Chaumont she expressed her fears:

Although Monsieur is somewhat softened, he still tells me there is only one way in which I can show my love for him. Such a remedy, you know, would be followed by certain death![14]

Did Henrietta truly fear for her safety at this point? Or was she being dramatic? She continued by having the hope that her husband would change:

Besides, the King has pledged his word that the Chevalier shall not return for eight years, by which time it is to be hoped Monsieur will either be cured of his passion, or else enlightened as to his favourite's true character. He may then see what faults this man had made him commit, and live to hate him as much as he once loved him. This is my only hope, although, even then, I may still be unhappy.[15]

The court set out for Flanders on 28 April. The king and queen were accompanied by the young Dauphin, Madame de Montespan, Louis' current mistress, Madame de Montpensier, La Grande Mademoiselle, hundreds of nobles of the court and 30,000 armed men. It was supposed to be a splendid procession but the torrential rain dampened the entourage. Approaching Landrécies, they found the river had burst its banks and forced them to spend a bedraggled night in an old barn with meagre provisions. The queen was disgusted but at least she wasn't outside in a makeshift tent like some of the other ladies.

Henrietta Anne wrote a quick letter to her friend before she left in which she told her 'Monsieur is still very angry with me, and I know that I shall have to expect many troubles, on my return'.[16] His attitude on the journey made for an uncomfortable ride. His constant unkind words riled the queen and La Grande Mademoiselle who were shocked when he told Henrietta that an astrologer had told him he would have many wives and since she was so ill, it would probably be soon. Although coping with the journey and anxious to see her brother, Henrietta had trouble with her stomach and could only drink asses milk. When the progress stopped for the day she immediately retired and slept as much as she could. But nothing would deter her from going to England and the work she was to undertake. The treaty was everything to her and she would see it through.

At Courtray she was met by English envoys who informed her Charles was ready and waiting at Dover as was Lord Sandwich who was waiting at Dunkirk with a fleet of ships to transport her across the water. Monsieur de Pomponne, the French ambassador at The Hague, also met her and along with the king and Monsieur accompanied her to Lille. The ambassador was suitably impressed.

I had a long conversation with her at Courtray and at Lisle, the evening before her departure, and I confess that I was astonished to find such grasp of mind and capacity for business, in a princess who seemed only born for the graces which are the ornament of her sex. I found that she was informed of the orders I had constantly had, not to enter into any solid alliance with the States, but to amuse them with useless negotiations. She knew the king's intentions to resent the part they had taken in the triple alliance, and showed great indignation at Temple for the dislike against France which he could not hide. However, she assured me that he would not long be in a condition to hurt us in this embassy. From what the king had said to me in general, about the hopes which he had of bringing back the King of England into his interests, and from what was confirmed to me by Madame, it was easy to guess that the voyage of this princess to London was not confined to the simple pleasure of seeing the king her brother.[17]

Henrietta sailed with 237 attendants including the Marshal du Plessis, Bishop of Tournay, Count and Countess de Grammont, Abbé Carnully, Abbé Chaumont, Monsieur l'Avocat, the Comte and Comtesse d'Albon, five maids of honour, among whom was Louise de Kérouaille, who would catch her brother's roving eye, seven ladies of the chamber, three maitres d'hôtel, a secretary, treasurer, physicians, and chaplains plus others.

On 24 May the weather was suitable for sailing. Charles was eagerly awaiting Henrietta along with their brother, James, the Duke of Monmouth and Prince Rupert. As soon as they spotted her ship, they sailed out in the royal barge to greet her. It had been nine years since she had stepped foot on English soil and now she was escorted to Dover Castle by her loving family. The castle being relatively small could only house some of her entourage and the rest had to spend their nights in accommodation found in the town.

Seeing as they only had three days together Charles wanted to get down to business straightaway. Negotiations began but then word came from Louis on the 31st that Henrietta Anne had permission to stay for ten or twelve days more. Still the treaty was her most important task and she spoke eloquently to her brother on its main points. She had always wished to see him convert to Catholicism and now with the backing of Louis, it was her role to convince him it would also be for the good of his nation. Charles could not concur on this point but still he agreed to it saying that for now he would not make public his wish to see England a Catholic country until the time was right. (It never would be and Charles would only convert to Catholicism on his deathbed.)

On the matter of Holland, they both agreed to war, with neither country allowed to negotiate peace with the Dutch without the other's consent. Louis was to attack by land, Charles by sea. Charles promised to supply 6000 troops and fifty warships. Louis would provide thirty ships, all to be under the command of the Duke of York. For his ongoing support, Louis would pay him 3,000,000 livres for every year of the war. For his conversion to Catholicism, Louis would supply him within three months 1,000,000 livres and a further 1,000,000 three months later to aid England's conversion. The treaty would swell England's coffers nicely.

The secret treaty of Dover was signed on 1 June by Colbert de Croissy on behalf of France and Lord Arundel, Lord Arlington, Sir Richard Bellings and Sir Thomas Clifford for England. Colbert de Croissy took the document to Louis who was waiting at Boulogne, received his signature and returned it to England. He reported to the king that 'it has seemed that Madame has more influence on her brother than any other person...'[18]

Henrietta Anne had done what she had set out to do and

finally she was triumphant at her part in bringing their, and her, two countries together. She could relax now and enjoy her visit. Although they were still in mourning for their mother, the siblings could enjoy each other's company. She met Queen Catherine for the first time 'a very good woman, not handsome, but so kind and excellent that it was impossible not to love her'[19] and they celebrated Charles' birthday in style. The Duchess of York also attended on her, anxious for news of her daughter who had joined Henrietta's household.

Philippe could do nothing to mar her pleasure over the next days. Although she was not allowed to go to London by her frustrating husband, she did go to Canterbury to see a ballet and comedy *The Sullen Lovers* by Thomas Shadwell. On 8 June the royals headed out in yachts to explore the coast accompanied by three man-of-wars. One of her ladies wrote 'Madame is as bold as she is on land and walks as fearlessly along the edge of ships as she does on shore'.[20] On their return a royal salute sounded from the guns at Dover castle.

These were delightful days, spending time with her brothers, but all too soon it was time to return to France. Charles gave her 6000 pistoles for her expenses and 2000 gold crowns to build a memorial chapel at Chaillot for their mother. He also gave her many jewels and Henrietta returning the favour asking her maid Louise de Kérouaille to bring in her jewel casket and offered him anything he would like. Charles, always on the lookout for lovely ladies, said he would take the maid and asked that she remain in England. Henrietta had to decline the giving of that gift.

Edmund Waller presented her with poem:

That sun of beauty did among us rise,
England first saw the light of your fair eyes;
In English, too, your early wit was shown;
Favour that language which was then your own:

When, tho' a child, through guards you made your way,
What fleet or army could an angel stay?
Thrice happy Britain l if she could retain
Whom she first bred within her ambient main. Our late-burnt
    London, in apparel new,
 Shook off her ashes to have treated you;
But we must see our glory snatched away,
And with warm tears increase the guilty sea:
No wind can favour us; howe'er it blows,
We must be wrack'd, and our dear treasure lose.
Sighs will not let us half our sorrows tell,
Fair, lovely, great, and best of nymphs, farewell.[21]

Henrietta Anne set sail on 12 June with her brothers accompanying part of the way. Charles was unable to let her go and said goodbye three times with profuse embraces. Henrietta was in tears as he finally left but before long the cannons of Calais were firing a welcome. She was back in France.

Louis XIV

Chapter Ten

A Royal Tragedy

1670

Henrietta Anne stayed the night in the governor's house at Calais and after attending mass the next morning set out for Boulogne. On her journey back to Paris she was accorded honours befitting her position. At Montreuil, the Duc d'Elboeuf laid on entertainments for her pleasure. Royal troops met her at Abbeville and escorted her to Beauvais where Sieur de Menevillette laid on an impressive welcome. Ralph Montagu, the English ambassador, who had not been part of the treaty negotiations, nevertheless had his suspicions. He met Henrietta at Beauvais to escort her to Saint-Germain and although she could not discuss the politics of her visit to England she gave him enough information to appease him. Rumours were spreading about the real reason for her visit.

Here is all the buzzing and rumour in the world that Madame hath had a secret negotiation with his majesty—that she hath made several presents at court, and at last prevailed, and that the triple alliance is quite to be broken; that indeed, for a colour, things are to be continued in their ancient channel for a little while, but that at last the disguise is to be taken off, and the King of England to unite publicly – with the King of France. These, because they are town news, and invented only to keep their tongues in use, it being an idle time and they having nothing else to busy themselves about, I think, therefore, the less notice is to be taken of them, for I do not question but his majesty is too well acquainted with his own interests not to forsake an alliance to which he himself gave the first favour, and of which he is still the greatest pillar and support, as that will be mutually to him, in case his affairs should require it.[1]

Henrietta Anne should have been greeted by the king and her husband en route but Philippe was refusing to ride out to meet her and Louis could not go without his brother. He finally deigned to meet Henrietta not far from Saint-Germain to escort her back to the palace where Louis was eagerly awaiting her. Delighted with her role in the treaty, he presented her with 6000 pistoles and asked her to move with the court to Versailles but Philippe would have none of it. Now she was back he wanted her to use her influence with Louis to free his lover Lorraine. Until she agreed she could expect to be kept away from court at their residence of St-Cloud. They spent a few days in Paris from where she wrote to Sir Thomas Clifford. She had asked Charles to give him a peerage and an earldom for Lord Arlington for their part in the treaty. It was the only letter she ever wrote in English.

> *When i have write to the King from Calais i praid him to tel milord Arlingtonan you what he had promised mi for bothe. his ansers was that hi gave me againe his word, that hee would performe the thing, but that hi did not thing it fit to exequte it now.*
>
> *I tel you this sooner than to Milord Arlingtonbecase i know you ar not so hard to satisfie as hee. I should be so my self, if I was not surethatvthe Kingwould not promismee a thing to faille in the performance of it.*
>
> *This is the ferste letter I have ever write in inglis. you will eselay see it bi the stile and tograf. prai see in the same timethat i expose mi self to be thought a foulle in looking to make you know how much I am your frind.*[2]

Henrietta was not without friends at Saint-Cloud. Madame de La Fayette rushed to welcome her home as did Turenne. Ralph Montagu visited her there as did Sir Thomas Armstrong and

Lord Paulett. She wrote to Madame de Saint-Chaumont on 26 June before heading to Versailles for the day. Philippe had not wanted to go but the king had ordered it.

She told her confidant:

Since my return, the King here has been very good to me, but as for Monsieur, nothing can equal his bitterness and anxiety to find fault. He does me the honour to say I am all-powerful, and can do everything I like, and so, if I do not bring back the Chevalier, it is because I do not wish to please him. At the same time he joins threats for the future with this kind of talk.[3]

She had returned to marital strife. Her journey home had been exhausting and she was tired and worn down with her husband's behaviour. Henrietta asked Madame de La Fayette to visit her. Her friendship would give her some consolation. Although she mentioned she had been suffering with a pain in her side, they talked late into the night in the peace and tranquillity of the gardens.

The next day she reiterated her distress to the Princess Palatine, her cousin by marriage who she tells 'I will confess that, on my return, I had hoped to find everyone satisfied, instead of which things are worse than ever'. She continues 'I am never to expect to be restored to his good graces until I have given him back his favourite'.[4] The letter is full of her troubles with Philippe and his insistence on having his lover back. The duke had asked her to raise him in Charles' estimation and urged her to ask Louis to give him his son's allowance. This she had done but for Lorraine, his fate lay with the king.

Towards the end of the letter she writes:

As for the Chevalier's return, even if my credit were as great as Monsieur believes it to be, I will never give way to blows. If Monsieur therefore refuses to accept the two things which he can have, and insists on getting the third, which must depend on the King's pleasure, I can only await the knowledge of Monsieur's will in silence. If he desires me to act I will do it joyfully, for I have no greater wish than to be on good terms with him. If not, I will keep silence and patiently bear all his unkindness, without trying to defend myself. His hatred is unreasonable, but his esteem may be earned. I may say that I have neither deserved the first, nor am I altogether unworthy of the last, and I still console myself with the hope that it may some day be obtained.[5]

But that day was not to come. Henrietta Anne wrote this letter on the last day of her life. Ralph Montagu would later send a copy to Charles acknowledging its authenticity.

She wrote the letter during a busy morning when she spent some time with her husband and then attended Mass with Madame de La Fayette. Afterwards she watched as an artist painted a portrait of her eldest daughter Marie Louise and at 11 o'clock they all sat down to eat together. Henrietta ate well but was tired early in the afternoon when she sat at Madame de La Fayette's feet on several cushions and placing her head in her lap went to sleep. Both Monsieur and Madame remarked that she didn't look well and when she woke she complained of stomach pains. She asked for a glass of chicory water to be brought to her. Her lady Madame de Gourdon knew a concentrate and fresh water to distil it was kept nearby in a closet. Henrietta had often taken it for stomach complaints. Her lady poured the drink into a silver cup for her but as soon as Henrietta drunk it she collapsed in pain crying out she had been poisoned. Her ladies rushed to her side, unlaced her gown and helped her to bed, trying to make her as comfortable as possible while she writhed in agony. Her doctor was called who diagnosed an acute attack of colic. Henrietta knew she was dying and asked for her husband telling him 'Alas, Monsieur, for a long time past you have not loved me; but that was unjust, for I have never failed you.'[6] She obviously believed that he had taken steps towards her demise.

Madame de La Fayette wrote in her account of Henrietta's final hours that Monsieur suggested that if she thought she had been poisoned they had better give some of the chicory water to a dog to test it. She also wrote that Madame des Bordes, Henrietta's chief waiting woman, had tasted the mixture to no ill effect. Henrietta asked for oil and an antidote which was brought to her but just made her sick. She wanted her priest and he was sent for as well as other doctors who continued to try her with remedies that did nothing but upset her stomach more.

News of her state was sent to Paris and before long the King and Queen arrived with several ladies from court. La Grande Mademoiselle thought Henrietta Anne looked like a corpse already but the king hugged her and wept uncontrollable tears at her pain. When he had composed himself, he suggested other treatments but her doctors by now could see there was no remedy for this illness. The priest came from Saint-Cloud as did the Jansenist priest, Monsieur Feuillet, but Henrietta wanted her old friend, Bossuet and he too was duly sent for. Others came to her bedside. Treville, who had loved her from afar and the Marechal de Gramont, the Comte de Guiche's father. Henrietta said a few words to them all.

Ralph Montagu hurried to her bedside. She told him 'You see, I am dying. Alas! How much I grieve for the King, my brother! He is losing the person who loves him best in the whole world'.[7] He was horrified to see her taken so low and speaking in English asked her if she had been poisoned. A maid supposedly heard her say 'If this is true you must never let the King, my brother, know of it. Spare him the grief at all events and do not let him take revenge on the King here for he is at least not guilty'.[8] Montagu was concerned for her private papers to Charles and a maid was sent to retrieve them but Monsieur had got there first. Henrietta gave her ring to the ambassador to pass on to her brother and offered him the 6000 pistoles Charles had given her in England but he refused to take the money and said he would give it to her servants. Everyone was now convinced she had little time left.

As Monsieur Feuillet spoke to her of sin and penitence, he was interrupted by the arrival of Bossuet who knelt by her side and asked her 'Madame, you believe in God, you hope in God, you love God?' She replied 'With all my heart'[9] as he intoned a final prayer and at three in the morning Henrietta died at just twenty-six years old.

King Louis was told the news when he woke and was sorely grieved. He wrote to tell Charles:

> My brother, The tender love I had for my sister was well known to you, and you will understand the grief into which her death has plunged me. In this heavy affliction, I can only say that the part which I take in your own sorrow, for the loss of one who was so dear to both of us, increases the burden of my regret. My only comfort is the confidence I cherish that this fatal accident will make no change in our friendship, and that you will continue to let me enjoy yours as fully as I give you mine.[10]

Given the suspicion of poison, Louis was aware that this could ruin the new relationship between France and England so he ordered a post-mortem. It took place that evening undertaken by two French doctors and two English with Montagu and a hundred other people present. The French doctors ruled she had died of cholera morbus but the English doctors felt that the post-mortem had not been performed to their satisfaction. One of them, Boscher, thought he had seen a hole in her stomach which he was not allowed to examine but nonetheless they all signed the death certificate wary of the political climate that hung heavily over the proceedings. The certificate, ended after a discussion of her body parts, with 'So that it was very boiling bile, very corrupt and malign, and very impetuous, which caused all the disorders in the abovesaid parts, and gangrened them'.[11]

Louis was not convinced and ordered Morel Simon, head of the Duke and Duchesses' household to tell him truthfully whether she had been poisoned. He thought she had but not by her husband. He saw the influence of Lorraine, still in Italy, but with two of his men, d'Effiat and Beuvron, living in the household and those he believed were responsible for her demise. Later Philippe's second wife would also believe Henrietta had been poisoned but not by her husband. She placed the blame on d'Effiat, 'one of Lucifer's subjects',[12] saying he had been seen near the closet in which Henrietta's chicory water was kept.

The chronicler, the Duc de Saint Simon, also saw d'Effiat as the culprit:

On the 29th of June, 1670, passing through this anteroom, he found the opportunity he sought; nobody was there, and he had re marked that nobody was following him to Madame's. He turned aside, went to the press, opened it, and threw in his 'powder; then hearing some one coming, took hold of the other pitcher, and as he was putting it back, the page of the chamber, who had the care of the chicory water, cried out, ran to him, and asked him sharply what he was doing in that press. D'Effiat, without the slightest embarrassment, asked par don, and said that he was dying with thirst, and that knowing that there was water there, pointing to the pitcher of common water, he had gone to drink.[13]

The problem with these reports is that their writers were not present at the time but wrote years later. Madame de La Fayette who was there ends Henrietta's memoirs with her death and does not discuss its cause. She did mention that Montagu had asked Henrietta if she had been poisoned but she didn't know if she had answered whether she had been. The English ambassador was however convinced and would always believe Henrietta had been poisoned. He wrote to Arlington immediately after her death to inform him. Days later, Arlington wrote to William Temple, the English ambassador at The Hague, to give him the news saying 'The Feuds amongst her Domesticks, and her sudden Death, made us, at first, believe that she was poyson'd; but the Account they have since given us of the great Care that was taken in examining her Corps, and the Sentiments of his Majesty... whose Interest it was to examine the Affair to the bottom, being fully of Opinion, that she dy'd a natural Death, has remov'd the greatest part of our Doubts'.[14] He at least was satisfied with a natural explanation for Henrietta's death.

Montagu asked for an audience with Louis and explained about her personal correspondence to her brother now being in her husband's hands. He asked that the letters to Charles be returned. He was not sure how sensitive they were but undoubtedly some would discuss politics and the recent treaty. Louis immediately ordered Philippe to relinquish them and they were sent on to England.

For Philippe's part he did not appear to be greatly affected by his wife's death and was more concerned with dressing himself and his daughters in extravagant mourning clothes. His cousin, La Grande Mademoiselle wrote in her memoirs:

I went to see Monsieur, who did not appear to me to be sorrowful. He told me that he had begged Madame d'Aiguillon to lend him her house at Ruel, for that in his situation he could not stay at Paris. The next day I returned with a mantle on to see Mademoiselle: there was there a daughter of the Duke of York, who had been sent to the queen mother of England to be put under treatment for a complaint which she had in her eyes; when the queen died she had remained under Madame's care. I found her with Mademoiselle: they were both very little. Monsieur, who loves fashions, had made them put on mantles which trailed on the ground: he wished that visits should be paid to Mademoiselle de Valois, although she was still a nursling. I went with my mantle to St. Germains; it was on purpose to see their majesties once with this ridiculous mourning trapping on. I told the king about the visits I had paid at the Palais Royal, and described to him the mantles of Mademoiselle and the Princess of England. He said to me, "Do not make nonsense about that, my brother would never forgive you."[15]

When Charles heard the devastating news of his much loved sisters' death he cried out 'Monsieur is a villain'.[16] The duke of Buckingham wanted war declared on France immediately. When the people heard the news they too cried out 'Death to the French!' and French men across the city were in fear of retribution. The French ambassador was sent a group of King's Guards to protect him. So in England too it was felt that Henrietta Anne had been murdered. But in honour of Henrietta's role in the secret treaty of Dover and the peace it had brought their countries, Charles could not retaliate. He shut himself away for five days when he must have considered the implications of accusing Lorraine or Philippe of murder. It would destroy the treaty and could lead them to the brink of war.

Louis could not afford the scandal nor the political implications. For now he ordered a state funeral for his beloved sister-in-law. Henrietta Anne left Saint-Cloud on 4 July at midnight to be taken to the abbey at Saint-Denis where the funeral was held six weeks later.

Much trouble had been taken to prepare the abbey. It was decorated as sumptuously as the ballets and plays Henrietta had so enjoyed in life. Black velvet was draped around the nave supported by seven foot high skeletons and four foot high candles lit the choir illuminating the figures of Youth, Nobility, Poetry and Music. 'The first was clothed in a rich mantle wrought with leopards and fleur-de-lys, a sceptre in her hand, and two crowns near her to denote the high birth of the princess; the second, lightly and delicately clad, held a broken garland, to denote that the illustrious deceased had passed away in the finest days of her spring time; the third was dressed as a nymph, crowned with laurel, and many books scattered at her feet; the fourth similarly attired, with a variety of instruments also at her feet... representing the fondness of the princess for the arts of music and poetry and her knowledge of them'.[17] Faith, Hope, Strength and Sweetness were also represented.

A platform with urns at each corner emitting incense was the base for an imitation black marble tomb on which her coffin was placed supported by bronze-coloured leopards. The coffin was draped with cloth of gold, trimmed with ermine, decorated with the arms of France and England, and on top sat her ducal mantle and coronet.

Louis did not attend the funeral nor did Monsieur but the queen was there as was Montagu and the duke of Buckingham. The three principal mourners were the Princess of Condé, the Duchess of Longueville and the Princess of Carignan, who were led into the abbey by the Prince of Condé, the Duke d'Enghien, and the Prince of Conti. The Archbishop of Rheims began the Mass while the principal mourners made their offerings. The four Bishops of Marseilles, Couserans, Meaux and Autun took part but it was Bishop Bossuet, her friend to the last, who had spoken such a splendid oration at her mother's funeral, who now did Henrietta proud with his eloquent speech:

This princess, born upon a throne, had a heart and a spirit even higher than her birth. The misfortunes of her house could not subdue her, even in her early youth; and from that time a grandeur was seen in her which owed nothing to fortune. She said with joy that heaven had snatched her, as by miracle, from the hands of the enemies of the king her father to give her to France. Precious gift! inestimable present! would that the possession had but been more lasting. But why does this recollection ever interrupt me? Alas! we cannot for a moment steady our gaze on the glory of the princess, without death blending with it to dim all with his shadow.

Oh death! Oh disastrous night! oh fearful night! When all at once resounded like a thunder clap the amazing tidings, 'Madame is dying; Madame is dead l' which of us did not feel himself smitten with this blow, as though some tragic accident had desolated his own family. At the first report of so strange a calamity, everybody flew to St. Cloud; all were in consternation, except the heart of this princess; everywhere cries were heard, everywhere was seen grief, despair, and the image of death. Monsieur, all the court, all the people, all were overwhelmed, all in despair, and we seem to see the accomplishment of those words of the prophet, 'The king shall weep, the prince shall be desolate, and the hands of the people shall fail with grief and astonishment.'[18]

Monsieur's bodyguards carried the coffin to the vault where her mother lay. Members of her household broke their staves and badges of office placing them within. Her ducal mantle and then her coronet was brought forward and 'All performed these functions not without bursting into tears at finding themselves deprived for ever of so charming and perfect a princess, and those of the company also, taking part in this sad concert of sighs and tears, gave marks and testimonies of extraordinary grief'.[19] Her heart was taken to the Abbey of Val de Grâce and her intestines to the church at Saint-Cloud where further services were conducted.

Henrietta Anne was mourned by many on both sides of the water. Bussy said after her death, 'She had more greatness and delicacy of taste, in things of the mind, than all the Ladies of the Court put together, and her death is therefore an infinite loss'.[20] Some felt her loss so keenly they left court, Treville and Madame de La Fayette included. Her great friend Daniel Cosnac also could not bear to be a part of a French court so much affected by her death and so much quieter for it. He wrote 'since men have been known to die of grief, it seems a crime on my part to have survived that day... with her I lost all hope or desire of returning to Court, and sick of the world, I turned my whole heart towards my sacred ministry'.[21] The shock and sorrow people felt at Henrietta Anne's death, the last of Charles I's daughters, would stay with them throughout their own lifetimes.

The Stuart princesses lived complicated lives in turbulent times. Apart from Anne who had died so young, all of them suffered great unhappiness as well as moments of joy. Poor Elizabeth never had the chance of a married life and children and died too young, separated from her family. Mary and Henrietta Anne had had the chance to be reunited with those they loved before their deaths but for these remarkable women their lives ended way too soon.

Appendix One

Those Henrietta Anne Left Behind

The king of France allowed the Chevalier de Lorraine to return from exile eighteen months after Henrietta Anne's death. Montagu wrote to Arlington at the time 'if Madame were poyson'd, as it is believ'd by most, all France look upon him for the person who did it, and is astonish'd, not without Reason, that the King of France should have so little Consideration for our Master, as to permit the Chevalier to come to court, especially, since he always behav'd himself in so Insolent a Manner toward the Princess, whilst she was living'.[1] Montagu would never forgive Lorraine and would be convinced of his involvement all his life. Academics now believe that Henrietta Anne may have succumbed to peritonitis caused by a duodenal ulcer but the case is still strong for poison administered by one of Lorraine's lackeys.

Louis was trying his best to quash the lingering rumours that Henrietta had been poisoned. By showing Lorraine was back in his brother's favour if not his, it underlined that the Duchess had died a natural death, for a murderer would not be welcome back at court. Louis would miss the radiant princess and it was said that the king never danced again in a ballet without his Henrietta to dance with him.

The men who had played a part in Henrietta Anne's life all survived her by many years. Charles II would reign for twenty-five years more. Louise de Kérouaille, Henrietta's maid, became his mistress and chief liaison between himself and Louis. Whereas Henrietta had been seen as a go-between for the benefit of both France and England, Louise was looked on with suspicion. The people of England never liked her and referred to her as a French spy.

As per the Treaty of Dover England joined France in war against the Dutch. The third Anglo-Dutch war took place from April 1672 to early 1674. As Louis marched his troops towards Holland for a land invasion, the English supported his actions with their navy. After naval battles at Sole Bay in 1672 and Ostend in 1673, England began to negotiate peace with the Dutch which was formalised with the Treaty of Westminster in February 1674.

Charles never did honour the secret, religious part of the treaty and convert England to Catholicism but from his death bed he spoke to a priest, receiving the last rites and finally joined his sister and mother's faith before he died on 6 February 1685. Louis, King of France, survived him by thirty years.

Philippe, Duke d'Orleans, remarried in November 1671. Elizabeth Charlotte of Bavaria, the only daughter of Charles Louis of the Elector Palatine and Charlotte of Hesse-Kassel, became his second wife to the relief of La Grande Mademoiselle who thought Louis might have paired her off with her cousin. Where Henrietta Anne had been a slight, willowy figure of a woman, Elizabeth was a strapping, larger lady who enjoyed the hunt and strode around in her boots, crop in hand. Saint-Simon described her as being 'badly shaped, badly dressed and badly disposed'[2] but here was another woman raised in a different country with different customs and culture who just did not seem to fit into the sumptuousness of the French court as she said herself when she wrote 'I am so little fitted for France that my whole life in the court is passed in the greatest solitude'.[3] She was the next woman to have to put up with Lorraine in her household even though she still suspected him of having a part in Henrietta's demise. She had three children with Philippe achieved by his use of 'rosaries and holy medals draped in the appropriate places to perform the necessary act'[4] but after they agreed to forego marital relations and managed to live reasonably well with each other until Philippe's death in 1701, by which time he had seen the error of his relationship with Lorraine.

Elizabeth Charlotte can be commended for the love she gave to Henrietta Anne's daughters. She became their stepmother and was happy to take on the role, enjoying the time she spent with them. Marie Louise, the eldest, became a court favourite and was very close to Louis' son, the Dauphin. Some thought they might marry but Louis arranged her marriage to Charles II of Spain in order to cement an alliance between their countries. Marie had no wish to leave France and dreaded, as many princesses before her, having to leave her home to live in a foreign country as queen of Spain. Charles was also known to have severe physical and mental disabilities in contrast to the dashing Dauphin. With his protruding lower jaw and drooling tongue, Charles was not a handsome man nor an appealing husband.

Louis told Marie Louise that he could not have done more for a daughter of his own in arranging their marriage to which she replied 'But you could have done better for your niece'.[5] Although she remonstrated with her uncle the proxy wedding went ahead at the Palace of Fontainebleau on 30 August 1679. Louis Armand I, Prince of Conti stood in for Charles and afterwards Marie Louise spent time at the convent of Val de Grâce, where her mother's heart was interred before she left for Spain. Louis' parting words were 'Madame, I hope never to see you again; the greatest misfortune that could happen would be to see you once more in France'.[6] Her father accompanied her as far as Amboise trying desperately to cheer her up.

On 19 November 1679, the seventeen-year-old Marie Louise and eighteen-year-old Charles married at Quintanapalla, near Burgos, Spain. He did everything to make her life happy but she constantly yearned for France. Spanish etiquette was strict and confining. Elizabeth had been sorry to see her go and felt for her beloved stepdaughter writing 'I really pity that poor child for having to live there. The little dogs she took with her are her only comfort. She may not even smile in public, or speak to her old servants, and all her French maids have begged leave to come home'.[7]

Her maids were in fact on the receiving end of anti-French feeling and Marie fared no better. She regularly wrote to her father of her unhappiness and loneliness. The Spanish did not take to their French queen. She tried hard to do as Louis had wished and promote France's interests but the court at Madrid conspired against her, spreading rumours of plots and intrigue so that she was never trusted. When she could she escaped to the Palacio del Buen Retiro from where she could ride out across the countryside on one of her French horses. It was a brief respite from her joyless life.

Marie Louise longed for children but it was not to be. She felt they would have added some happiness to her long lonely days. Given the inbreeding of her husband's family he was probably impotent and he would never father any heirs of Spain. Before long Marie fell into a lasting depression and consoled herself with comfort food and overeating. On February 11 1689 after nearly ten years of marriage she took to bed with stomach pains like her mother had done. And when she died rumours also talked of poison. The finger was pointed at the Comtesse de Soissons, Henrietta's old enemy and now Marie's lady, but nothing was ever proved. Her husband mourned her greatly as did the French court when they heard the news. Louis is said to have left the room in tears.

Anne Marie – Henrietta and Philippe's second daughter – had hardly known her mother and Elizabeth Charlotte was to play a central role in her life as the maternal figure. She was married at the age of fourteen to Victor Amadeus II of Savoy, then Duke of Savoy, later King of Sicily and then of Sardinia, who was three years older. Their proxy marriage was held at Versailles on 10 April 1684 with her cousin, Louis-Auguste de Bourbon, duc du Maine standing in as bridegroom. Her father escorted her only a little way on her journey to Savoy, just as far as Juvisy outside of

Paris, saddened by taking leave of his last daughter by Henrietta Anne.

On 6 May 1684, Anne Marie and Victor were married at Chambéry by the Archbishop of Grenoble. Two days later, they made their state entry into Turin where Anne Marie would take up residence in the royal palace. Elizabeth Charlotte would write to her every week and eagerly awaited her return letters. As well as staying at the palace, Anne Marie also spent her time at the Vigna di Madama Reale and the Palazzina di caccia di Stupinigi. She was more at home in Savoy, now part of Italy, than her sister had been in Spain and soon found a friend in her mother-in-law, Marie Jeanne, who had acted as regent for her son up until his marriage. Victor was not impressed feeling his pro-French mother meddled too much in political affairs that should be left up to him and was jealous of his wife's relationship. Neither was Anne Marie particularly happy with him after finding out about his mistresses and illegitimate children.

Anne Marie had nine children throughout the course of their marriage but only three lived to adulthood – Marie-Adélaïde, Maria Luisa and Charles Emmanuel. She gave birth to her first child Marie-Adélaïde in 1685 at the age of sixteen which nearly killed her. The birth was so traumatic she was given last rites but pulled through.

Her daughter Maria Luisa was married at thirteen to the new King Philip of Spain in 1701. The death of the childless Charles II, previously married to Anne Marie's sister, had caused concern over the Spanish succession when he left the crown to his grandnephew and Louis' grandson Philip, Duke of Anjou. The war of succession that followed saw Victor siding with the Austrians against France and Spain. Anne Marie was caught in the middle with British and French relatives fighting on opposing sides.

Anne Marie was left to act as regent of Savoy whilst Victor joined the war. It would continue for many years and in 1706,

Turin was the battle ground of French troops under the command of her half-brother Philippe d'Orléans, Elizabeth Charlotte's son, and Philip V's Spanish force. Fleeing for their lives, they found sanctuary in Genoa.

The war ended in 1713 and Victor Amadeus was made King of Sicily, formerly a Spanish possession. Anne Marie joined him there for their coronation and Elizabeth Charlotte was delighted 'I shall neither gain nor lose by the peace, but one thing I shall enjoy is to see our Duchess of Savoy become a queen, because I love her as though she were my own child'.[8] Victor would later have to give up Sicily but received the kingdom of Sardinia instead.

Anne Marie had a claim to the thrones of England, Scotland and Ireland in her own right from 1714 to 1720. When Queen Anne died in 1714 she became heir presumptive through her mother's Stuart blood and the claim of Prince James Francis Edward Stuart, the queen's brother. Queen Anne, daughter of James, Duke of York and king after Charles II's death, was the little girl that had been sent to live with Henrietta Anne and her mother due to an eye complaint but she had returned to England after Henrietta's death. She was a popular queen and had reigned with her husband George of Denmark from 1702. None of her children survived her and due to the Act of Settlement of 1701 Catholics were prohibited from inheriting the British throne. This meant that Prince James' claim and Anne Marie as his heir was passed over to Queen Anne's closest living Protestant relative, George, Prince of Hanover. In 1720, Prince James also had a son who would become 'Bonnie Prince Charlie', thus ruling Anne Marie out of the English succession.

Anne Marie's eldest daughter Marie-Adélaïde had married Louis, Duke of Burgundy, grandson of Louis XIV in 1697 at the age of eleven and left Turin to be brought up in France. In 1715 her son became King Louis XV of France.

Anne Marie died the day before her fifty-ninth birthday of

heart failure on 26 August 1728 and was buried at the Basilica of Superga in Turin.

Henrietta Anne's descendants would continue to pass on their Stuart blood to the royal houses of Europe. These included King Felipe VI of Spain, King Philippe of the Belgians, Grand Duke Henri of Luxembourg, Henri, Count of Paris, the Orléanist pretender to the French throne, and Victor Emmanuel of Savoy, the pretender to the Italian throne.

References

Prologue
1. King Charles speech
2. Ibid.
3. Ibid.
4. Lisle, *Charles I*

Chapter One
1. Lockyer, *Buckingham*
2. Hamilton, *Henrietta Maria*
3. Ibid.
4. Hutchinson, *Memoirs of the Life of Colonel Hutchinson*
5. Tillières, *Memoires*
6. Ibid.
7. Whitaker, *A Royal Passion*
8. *CSP Venice*
9. Laing, *The History of Scotland*
10. Gaunt, *The English Civil Wars*
11. Everett Green, *Lives of the Princesses of England*
12. Plowden, *The Stuart Princesses*
13. Everett Green, *Lives of the Princesses of England*
14. Plowden, *The Stuart Princesses*
15. *CSP Venice*
16. D'Ewes, *Journal*
17. Hamilton, *Henrietta Maria*
18. *CSP Venice*
19. Porter, *Royal Renegades*
20. Ferrero, *Lettres de Henriette Marie*
21. Coates, *The Private Journals of the Long Parliament*
22. Everett Green, *Letters*
23. Strickland, *Lives of the Last Four Princesses*
24. Everett Green, *Lives of the Princesses of England*

25. Ibid.
26. Hamilton, *Henrietta Maria*

Chapter Two

1. Everett Green, *Lives of the Princesses of England*
2. Ibid.
3. Plowden, *Henrietta Maria*
4. Ibid.
5. Norrington, *My Dearest Minette*
6. Ibid.
7. Porter, *Royal Renegades*
8. Cartwright, *Madame: A life of Henrietta*
9. Ibid.
10. Ibid.
11. Plowden, *Henrietta Maria*
12. Strickland, *Lives of the Last Four Princesses*
13. Cartwright, *Madame: A life of Henrietta*
14. Rivington, *Eikōn Basilikē*
15. Everett Green, *Lives of the Princesses of England*
16. Ibid.
17. Strickland, *Lives of the Last Four Princesses*
18. Cartwright, *Madame: A life of Henrietta*
19. Ibid.
20. Everett Green, *Lives of the Princesses of England*
21. Spencer, *Prince Rupert*
22. Norrington, *My Dearest Minette*
23. Cartwright, *Madame: A life of Henrietta*
24. Ibid.
25. Norrington, *My Dearest Minette*
26. Montpensier, *Memoirs of Mademoiselle de Montpensier*
27. Ibid.
28. Plowden, *Henrietta Maria*
29. Everett Green, *Lives of the Princesses of England*
30. Plowden, *Henrietta Maria*

Chapter Three

1. Everett Green, *Lives of the Princesses of England*
2. Ibid.
3. Porter, *Royal Renegades*
4. Clarke, *The Life of James the Second*
5. Cartwright, *Madame: A life of Henrietta*
6. Ibid.
7. Norrington, *My Dearest Minette*
8. Strickland, *Lives of the Last Four Princesses*
9. Hargrave, *A Complete Collection of State Trials*
10. Plowden, *Henrietta Maria*
11. Everett Green, *Lives of the Princesses of England*
12. Cary, *Memorials the Great Civil War*
13. Ibid.
14. Porter, *Royal Renegades*
15. Petitot (ed.), *Memoiries*
16. *CSP Venice*
17. Stedman, *Cultural Exchange in Seventeenth-Century France and England*
18. Ibid.
19. Plowden, *Henrietta Maria*
20. Fraser, *King Charles II*
21. *The Journal of the British Archaeological Association*
22. Hamilton, *Henrietta Maria*
23. Strickland, *Lives of the Last Four Princesses*
24. Porter, *Royal Renegades*
25. Strickland, *Lives of the Last Four Princesses*
26. Ibid.
27. Rait, *Five Stuart Princesses*
28. Plowden, *Henrietta Maria*
29. Cartwright, *Madame: A life of Henrietta*
30. Wilkinson, *Louis XIV*
31. Strickland, *Lives of the Last Four Princesses*
32. Ibid.

33. Everett Green, *Lives of the Princesses of England*

Chapter Four

1. Wilson, *Love in Letters*
2. Strickland, *Lives of the Last Four Princesses*
3. Warner, *Nicholas Papers*
4. Norrington, *My Dearest Minette*
5. Cartwright, *Madame: A life of Henrietta*
6. Everett Green, *Lives of the Princesses of England*
7. Ibid.
8. Ibid.
9. Oman, *The Winter Queen*
10. Everett Green, *Lives of the Princesses of England*
11. Strickland, *Lives of the Last Four Princesses*
12. Everett Green, *Lives of the Princesses of England*
13. Ibid.
14. Plowden, *Henrietta Maria*
15. Ibid.
16. Montpensier, *Memoirs of Mademoiselle de Montpensier*
17. Plowden, *Henrietta Maria*
18. Strickland, *Lives of the Last Four Princesses*
19. Everett Green, *Lives of the Princesses of England*
20. Ibid.
21. Cartwright, *Madame: A life of Henrietta*

Chapter Five

1. Everett Green, *Lives of the Princesses of England*
2. Norrington, *My Dearest Minette*
3. Ibid.
4. Ibid.
5. Ibid.
6. Plowden, *The Stuart Princesses*
7. Rait, *Five Stuart Princesses*
8. Everett Green, *Lives of the Princesses of England*

9. Rait, *Five Stuart Princesses*
10. Hartman, *Charles II and Madame*
11. *CSP Venice*
12. Cartwright, *Madame: A life of Henrietta*
13. Norrington, *My Dearest Minette*
14. Everett Green, *Lives of the Princesses of England*
15. Ibid.
16. Bevan, *Charles the II's Minette*
17. Pepys, *The Diary of Samuel Pepys*
18. Strickland, Agnes, *Lives of the Queens of England*
19. *CSP Venice*
20. Strickland, *Lives of the Last Four Princesses*
21. Rait, *Five Stuart Princesses*
22. Strickland, *Lives of the Last Four Princesses*
23. Ibid.
24. Wilkinson, *Louis XIV*
25. Cartwright, *Madame: A life of Henrietta*
26. Bevan, *Charles the II's Minette*
27. Cartwright, *Madame: A life of Henrietta*
28. Ibid.
29. Ibid.
30. Hartman, *Charles II and Madame*

Chapter Six

1. Hartman, *Charles II and Madame*
2. Cartwright, *Madame: A life of Henrietta*
3. Ibid.
4. Norrington, *My Dearest Minette*
5. Ibid.
6. Ibid.
7. Cartwright, *Madame: A life of Henrietta*
8. Everett Green, *Lives of the Princesses of England*
9. Bevan, *Charles the II's Minette*
10. Ibid.

11. Norrington, *My Dearest Minette*
12. Everett Green, *Lives of the Princesses of England*
13. Norrington, *My Dearest Minette*
14. Cartwright, *Madame: A life of Henrietta*
15. Ibid.
16. Everett Green, *Lives of the Princesses of England*
17. Cartwright, *Madame: A life of Henrietta*

Chapter Seven

1. Norrington, *My Dearest Minette*
2. Cartwright, *Madame: A life of Henrietta*
3. Ibid.
4. Ibid.

Chapter Eight

1. Cartwright, *Madame: A life of Henrietta*
2. Ibid.
3. Norrington, *My Dearest Minette*
4. Ibid.
5. Bevan, *Charles the II's Minette*
6. Cartwright, *Madame: A life of Henrietta*
7. Bevan, *Charles the II's Minette*
8. Plowden, *The Stuart Princesses*
9. Norrington, *My Dearest Minette*
10. Ibid.

Chapter Nine

1. Norrington, *My Dearest Minette*
2. Bevan, *Charles the II's Minette*
3. Ibid.
4. Cartwright, *Madame: A life of Henrietta*
5. Norrington, *My Dearest Minette*
6. Hartman, *Charles II and Madame*
7. Norrington, *My Dearest Minette*

8. Cartwright, *Madame: A life of Henrietta*
9. Fraser, *King Charles II,*
10. Everett Green, *Lives of the Princesses of England*
11. Cartwright, *Madame: A life of Henrietta*
12. Ibid.
13. Norrington, *My Dearest Minette*
14. Ibid.
15. Ibid.
16. Cartwright, *Madame: A life of Henrietta*
17. Everett Green, *Lives of the Princesses of England*
18. Bevan, *Charles the II's Minette*
19. Cartwright, *Madame: A life of Henrietta*
20. Bevan, *Charles the II's Minette*
21. *Book of the Poets: Chaucer to Beattie*

Chapter Ten
1. Everett Green, *Lives of the Princesses of England*
2. Norrington, *My Dearest Minette*
3. Plowden, *The Stuart Princesses*
4. Cartwright, *Madame: A life of Henrietta*
5. Ibid.
6. Madame de la Fayette, *The Secret History of Henrietta*
7. Cartwright, *Madame: A life of Henrietta*
8. Norrington, *My Dearest Minette*
9. Cartwright, *Madame: A life of Henrietta*
10. Ibid.
11. Everett Green, *Lives of the Princesses of England*
12. McLaughlin, *The Second Madame*
13. Everett Green, *Lives of the Princesses of England*
14. Madame de la Fayette, *The Secret History of Henrietta*
15. Montpensier, *Memoirs of Mademoiselle de Montpensier*
16. Jordan & Walsh, *The King's Bed*
17. Everett Green, *Lives of the Princesses of England*
18. Ibid.

19. Ibid.
20. Cartwright, *Madame: A life of Henrietta*
21. Ibid.

Appendix

1. Madame de la Fayette, *The Secret History of Henrietta*
2. Cartwright, *Madame: A life of Henrietta*
3. McLaughlin, *The Second Madame*
4. Fraser, *King Charles II*
5. Nichols Barker, *Brother to the Sun King*
6. Ibid.
7. Cartwright, *Madame: A life of Henrietta*
8. Orleans, *Letters from Liselotte*

Bibliography

Airy, Osmund, *Charles II*, London, 1904

Ashley, Maurice, *The Stuarts In Love*, London, 1963

Bevan, Bryan, *Charles the II's Minette*, London, 1979

Bevan, Bryan, *Charles the Second's French Mistress*, London, 1972

Book of the Poets: Chaucer to Beattie, London, 1842

Bryant, Arthur, *Restoration England*, London, 1960

Burnet, Gilbert, *History of His Own Times*, 6 vols, London, 1833

Calendar of State Papers, Domestic – Charles II

Calendar of State Papers, Venice

Cartwright, Julia, *Madame: A life of Henrietta, daughter of Charles I. and Duchess of Orleans*, London, 1894

Cary Henry (ed), *Memorials the Great Civil War in England, from 1641-1652*, London, 1842

Clarke, *The Life of James the Second*, London, 1816

Coates, Young and Snow (eds), *The Private Journals of the Long Parliament: 3 January to 5 March 1642*, London, 1982

Davidson, Lillias Campbell, *Catherine of Braganca, Infanta of Portugal and Queen-Consort of England*, London, 1908

D'Ewes, Sir Simonds, *The Journal of Sir Simonds D'Ewes: From the Beginning of the Long Parliament to the Opening of the Trial of the Earl of Strafford*, London, 1923

Elsna, Hebe, *Catherine of Braganza: Charles II's Queen*, London, 1967

Evelyn, John, *The Diary of John Evelyn*, (kindle edition) Los Angeles, 2009

Everett Green, Mary Anne, *Letters of Queen Henrietta Maris: Including her Private Correspondence with Charles the First*, London, 1857

Everett Green, Mary Anne, *Lives of the Princesses of England: From the Norman Conquest, Volume 6*, London, 1855

Ferrero, H, *Lettres de Henriette Marie a sa Soeur Christine*, Rome,

1881

Fraser, Antonia, *King Charles II*, London, 2002

Fraser, Antonia, *The Weaker Vessel*, London, 1984

Gaunt, Peter, *The English Civil Wars 1642 – 1651*, Oxford, 2003

Graham, Hinds, Hobby & Wilcox (eds), *Her Own Life: autobiographical writings by seventeenth-century Englishwomen*, London, 1989

Hargrave, Francis (ed), *A Complete Collection of State Trials*, Dublin, 1793

Hartman, Cyril Hughes, *La Belle Stuart*, London, 1924

Hartman, Cyril Hughes, *Charles II and Madame*, London, 1934

Hamilton, Elizabeth, *Henrietta Maria*, London, 1976

Hanrahan, David, *Charles II and the Duke of Buckingham*, Stroud, 2006

Hanson, Neil, *The Great Fire of London*, New York, 2002

Hopkins, Graham, *Constant Delights: Rakes, rogues and scandal in Restoration England*, London, 2002

Howitt, Mary Botham, *Biographical Sketches of the Queens of Great Britain*, London, 1862

Hutchinson, Lucy, *Memoirs of the Life of Colonel Hutchinson; With Original Anecdotes of Many of the Most Distinguished of His Contemporaries, and a Summary Review of Public Affairs*, London, 1822

Jordan D & Walsh M, *The King's Bed: Sex, Power and the Court of Charles II*, London, 2015

Kenyon, J P, *Stuart England*, London, 1978

King Charls, His Speech, Made upon the Scaffold at Whitehall-Gate, Immediately before his Execution, On Tuesday the 30 of Ian. 1648, London, 1649

Laing, Malcolm, *The history of Scotland, from the union of the crowns, to the union of the kingdoms*, London, 1804

Lisle, Leanda de, *Charles I: Traitor, Murderer, Martyr*, London, 2018

Lockyer, Roger, *Buckingham: The Life and Political Career of George*

Villiers, First Duke of Buckingham, 1592-1628, London, 1981

Mackay, Janet, *Catherine of Braganza*, London, 1937

Madame de la Fayette, *The Secret History of Henrietta, Princess of England: First Wife of Philippe, Duc d'Orleans*, London, 1929

Masters, Brian, *The Mistresses of Charles II*, London, 1979

McLaughlin, M., *The Second Madame: A memoir of Elizabeth Charlotte, Duchess d'Orleans*, New York, 1895

Melville, Lewis, *The Windsor Beauties: Ladies of the Court of Charles II*, Michigan, 2005

Montpensier, Anne Marie Louise d'Orleans, *Memoirs of Mademoiselle de Montpensier: Grand-daughter of Henri Quatre, and Niece of Queen Henrietta-Maria*, London, 1848

Nichols Barker, Nancy, *Brother to the Sun King Philippe, Duke of Orléans*, Maryland, 1989

Norrington, Ruth, (ed) *My Dearest Minette: letters between Charles II and his sister, the Duchesse d'Orleans*, London, 1996

Ollrad, Richard, *Clarendon and His Friends*, Oxford, 1987

Oman, Carola, *The Winter Queen: Elizabeth of Bohemia*, London, 1938

Original Letters Illustrative of English History, London, 1824

Orléans (duchesse d'), Charlotte-Elisabeth, *Letters from Liselotte: Elisabeth Charlotte, Princess Palatine and Duchess of Orléans, 'Madame', 1652-1722*, London, 1970

Petitot, Claude Bernard, ed., *Collection des mémoires relatifs à l'histoire de France*, Paris, 1825

Pepys, *The Diary of Samuel Pepys*, ed. Latham & Matthews, 11 vols, 1970-83

Plowden, Alison, *Henrietta Maria: Charles I's Indomitable Queen*, Stroud, 2001

Plowden, Alison, *The Stuart Princesses*, Stroud, 1996

Porter, Linda, *Royal Renegades: The Children of Charles I and the English Civil Wars*, London, 2016

Porter, Stephen, *Pepy's London*, Stroud, 2012

Pritchard, R E, *Scandalous Liaisons: Charles II and his Court*,

Stroud, 2015

Rait, Robert, *Five Stuart Princesses*, London, 1902

Rivington C and J. (eds), *Eikōn Basilikē: The Pourtraicture of His Sacred Majestie in His Solitudes and Sufferings*, London, 1824

Spencer, Charles, *Prince Rupert: The Last Cavalier*, London, 2007

Stedman, Gesa, *Cultural Exchange in Seventeenth-Century France and England*, London, 2016

Strickland, Agnes, *Lives of the Last Four Princesses of the House of Stuart*, London, 1872

Strickland, Agnes, *Lives of the Queens of England*, London, 1847

The Journal of the British Archaeological Association, volume 11, 1885

Tillières, Comte Tanneguy Leveneur de, *Memoires Inedits du comte Leveneur de Tillières*, Paris, 1863

Trevelyan, G M, *England Under the Stuarts*, London, 1904

Uglow, Jenny, *A Gambling Man: Charles II and the Restoration*, London, 2009

Waller, Edmund, *The Triple Combat*, 1675

Warner, George F., (ed), *Correspondence of Sir Edward Nicholas (The Nicholas Papers)*, London, 1892

Wheatley, Dennis, *Old Rowley: A Very Private Life of Charles II*, London, 1962

Whittingham, C, (ed), *The British Poets*, Chiswick, 1822

Wilkinson, Richard, *Louis XIV*, London, 2017

Wilson, Derek, *All the King's Women: Love, sex and politics in the life of Charles II*, London, 2003

Wilson, James Grant, *Love in Letters*, London, 1867

Worden, Blair, *The English Civil Wars 1640–1660*, London, 2009

Chronos Books
HISTORY

Chronos Books is an historical non-fiction imprint. Chronos publishes real history for real people; bringing to life people, places and events in an imaginative, easy-to-digest and accessible way - histories that pass on their stories to a generation of new readers.
If you have enjoyed this book, why not tell other readers by posting a review on your preferred book site.

Recent bestsellers from Chronos Books are:

Lady Katherine Knollys
The Unacknowledged Daughter of King Henry VIII
Sarah-Beth Watkins
A comprehensive account of Katherine Knollys' questionable
paternity, her previously unexplored life in the Tudor court
and her intriguing relationship with Elizabeth I.
Paperback: 978-1-78279-585-8 ebook: 978-1-78279-584-1

Cromwell was Framed
Ireland 1649
Tom Reilly
Revealed: The definitive research that proves the Irish nation
owes Oliver Cromwell a huge posthumous apology for
wrongly convicting him of civilian atrocities in 1649.
Paperback: 978-1-78279-516-2 ebook: 978-1-78279-515-5

Why The CIA Killed JFK and Malcolm X
The Secret Drug Trade in Laos
John Koerner
A new groundbreaking work presenting evidence that the CIA
silenced JFK to protect its secret drug trade in Laos.
Paperback: 978-1-78279-701-2 ebook: 978-1-78279-700-5

The Disappearing Ninth Legion
A Popular History
Mark Olly
The Disappearing Ninth Legion examines hard evidence for the
foundation, development, mysterious disappearance, or possi-
ble continuation of Rome's lost Legion.
Paperback: 978-1-84694-559-5 ebook: 978-1-84694-931-9

Readers of ebooks can buy or view any of these bestsellers by clicking on the live link in the title. Most titles are published in paperback and as an ebook. Paperbacks are available in traditional bookshops. Both print and ebook formats are available online.

Find more titles and sign up to our readers' newsletter at
http://www.johnhuntpublishing.com/history-home

Follow us on Facebook at
https://www.facebook.com/ChronosBooks

and Twitter at https://twitter.com/ChronosBooks